First Holy Communion

MARK ALLEN

First Holy Communion

With a Foreword by
His Excellency Archbishop Giovanni Tonucci
Apostolic Nuncio in Kenya

Burns & Oates

This paperback edition published in 2002 by
BURNS & OATES
A Continuum imprint
The Tower Building
11 York Road
London SE1 7NX
www.continuumbooks.com

© Mark Allen 2002

British Library Cataloguing-in-Publication Data
A catalogue record for this book is available from the British
Library.

ISBN 0 86012 326 X (paperback)

Production editor, typesetting from author's disk, Bill Ireson
Printed in Great Britain by Biddles Limited, *www.biddles.co.uk*

Contents

surpasses understanding. Prayer. Contact with
God is in love: the offering of the heart.
Humility – the silence of the contrite heart. The
sacrifice of the self transcends ritual

Foreword

It gives me great joy to know that *First Holy Communion*, which Mark Allen prepared for the introduction of his own children to the sacrament of the Eucharist, is now to be published. It is a long time since that moment in Belgrade when he decided to take the responsibility of accompanying his son, Roly, in discovering and understanding the plan of God in his life. That decision, and the work of selection that resulted from it, still have enormous value.

At that time there were special reasons why he should have followed that course. I remember well the difficulties which families faced in instructing their children when living far away from their own countries. For more than one reason, there were few options for catechism courses in Belgrade, at least in English, and it was necessary to find some other solution. Today, too, since work overseas has become more and more usual, there are countless thousands of families which find themselves in the same situation.

But this justification is only partial. In fact, what at first sight might appear a sort of escape determined by external and temporary circumstances, revealed itself as an important element in the Christian education of a child with the parents themselves directly involved in it. It is not only the parents who find themselves in the special situation just described who will benefit from this book. All parents who feel that it is not sufficient for them to be passive witnesses in the human and religious education of their children, but who want to take part in a direct and personal way, will benefit.

The book in its published form is intended as an immediate help to those whose children are preparing for their first Holy Communion. It can be used as a practical guide for instruction. But perhaps its greatest usefulness will lie in providing parents with a framework for revising and reviewing their own thinking and approach to the sacrament of the Eucharist.

I hope that many will find help and encouragement in these pages, and it is my firm conviction that such renewal will be a strong stimulus to the children as they grow in the midst, and with the support, of their family.

† GIOVANNI TONUCCI
Apostolic Nuncio in Kenya

Acknowledgements

The passages from the Bible are taken from the 1966 version of the *Jerusalem Bible*, published and copyright 1966, 1967 and 1968 by Darton Longman and Todd Ltd and Doubleday & Co Inc, and are used by permission of the publishers.

References to the Catechism are to *Catechism of the Catholic Church*, published by Geoffrey Chapman 1994. The paragraphs in the Catechism are numbered and references are to the paragraph numbers: for example, 'Catechism, 1324'.

I am grateful to Mary Douglas who gave me permission to quote her, on page 32; to Penguin Books for their kind permission to reproduce, on page 146, the excerpt from John Marsh's *Saint John*, from the *Penguin New Testament Commentaries*, published in 1968; and to Crossroads Publishing for the source reference on page 155.

Author's Note

In this book, the passages from the Bible give some of the main parts in the story of revelation which culminates in the Paschal mystery of Jesus. These are the key parts for a child. Each passage may present its own difficulties, but as the story builds up, it will make its own sense and, perhaps more importantly, become an early part of the child's own self-awareness and awareness of the dimension of God in his or her own life. The reflections printed below the passages for reading, are meant in the greater part for the grown-up as material to get the mind thinking around the key themes. After thinking through different aspects of what these passages mean, it will be easier to speak to the child with conviction about the simpler and core themes which are needed at this stage. These last are printed in **bold** to make them easier to refer back to.

In Chapter 13, the passages from Luke printed in *italics* provide cross-references to books in the Old Testament, enabling readers to make the comparison.

Introduction

These pages had their beginning in a question, 'How do I prepare a child for first Holy Communion?' I faced this question when there was little help to hand and I had to try to answer it for myself. These pages started as notes for a course of instruction which I used myself with my own children. Later on others used them and said they found them useful, either directly in instructing their own children or for themselves alongside a course a child was following.

Using these notes, I reflected that really I was the one who first needed help and not the children. They were open whereas parts of me were closed to what I needed to say. Young children will take on trust whatever their parents tell them, so long as it is true and does not make them suspicious, does not offend their sense of what is fair. The success we have in putting it across is the measure of how much we ourselves are convinced of what we want to say. And that is the fundamental issue in instructing a child for first Holy Communion. Are we ourselves convinced? We take the children to Mass, but what are we about when we go to Mass ourselves? What really do we have to say about it? These pages offer readings and background from scripture and the catechism for considering how we, each in our own way, may answer that question. Thus they are really for the grown-up, but I think that they can also be a framework for instructing a child.

When I first asked myself, 'How do I prepare a child for first Holy Communion?' the problem was practical and immediate – 'What to do and do now?' Our eldest child was seven.

We were living abroad. There were very few Catholic priests, they hardly spoke English and were very busy. There were even fewer nuns and they had even less English. The problem of catechism and instruction loomed. With envy I remembered the well-ordered classes given by nuns I had been to when I was seven.

The foreign community in Belgrade where we were, gathered for Sunday Mass, said each week in a different European language. You could not but notice people in the community coming back to the Mass as their children came to the age for first Holy Communion. It was as though these tiny people with their spiritual enthusiasms, even if fired by thoughts of white dresses and presents, wanting to be included in this or that nationality's catechism class, were dragging their parents back to the practice of the faith. They pulled them to church like miniature tractors. In our case there were not many Catholic English-speaking children; there was no catechism class in English. I shared the thoughts on the faces of those returning to Mass: what was so familiar, now seemed again new. The children were making us look at things anew.

I asked for help from a young Papal diplomat who met my appeal with another question, a direct one. 'Why do you think that there can be someone else to do this for your child? Isn't this the most important service a parent can do for a child, to pass on the faith? Don't', he went on, 'be a conventional, a lukewarm Catholic and try to get the clergy or religious to do this for you. Do it yourself and it will do you good.' To be fair, he did say he would help. He would stay in touch and monitor progress. In the end he would examine our son and, if all went well, give him his first Holy Communion at the Nunciature. And that was what happened.

I began work laying out a course for my son. During a visit to London I looked for material in Catholic bookshops.

There was a variety to be had but, whatever its objective merits, it left me feeling distant and lonely. It just did not resonate with the way we talked at home, nor did it strike chords with my own understanding of my religion at that time. The hard core of doctrine which ought to have been common ground, did not seem to get much emphasis. There was not much the curious and energetic mind of a child could fix on. I bought a copy of the old 'penny' catechism to help my own revision and went back to the Bible.

I followed some simple principles. Children are hard-headed and like facts. They like stories. The narratives of the Bible would provide facts, events which happened, and along with them the objective truths of revelation. In framing simple explanations and drawing out the themes which would lead towards some understanding of the Eucharist, I would be using the language the child best understood, the language of his own home. In this way, I hoped I should also be saying that these narratives, themes and beliefs were also us, what we as a family tried to believe in, that they underlay our own understanding of ourselves, of our identity.

Most importantly, the Mass is our sacramental encounter with the person of Jesus. My preparation, therefore, should centre on him, be based on the Gospel story of his life. Rather differently from the way I had been instructed for first Holy Communion, I should try to bring catechism and scripture together. The preparation should reflect the unity of the Mass: its Liturgy of the Word and the Eucharistic Rite, the mystery of the real presence of Christ in our community as Church and as communion in our sacrament of the Eucharist.

I found, as also later with our second child, that routine was the key aid to progress. We never did more than half an hour at a go, but if – and those were fiercely busy days – we missed a session, we tried as best we could to make it up before the next. Each session was simple: we read the passages aloud to each other and talked about them. Somehow we managed without visual aids, cartoons or colouring-in. Having a date agreed in advance for the 'examination' by our new friend kept us at it.

Was this too difficult for us? Yes, it was quite difficult; but introducing a child to mysteries on which a soul may reflect all the days of its life, is bound to be a challenge. Life itself is not easy, but recognising and facing the challenges is more than half the coping with them. The Gospels have something to say to each of us at every stage in life. We find our own level and try to move on. We *are* moved on: we are carried by the Holy Spirit, as we reflect and grow.

The fundamental difficulty – and it is for us and not for the child – is the difficulty of faith. Do I have faith? How easy is it for us to answer that question? Shyness and inarticulacy about religion are the norm for us in our everyday lives. We usually avoid the topic in conversation with other adults. We do not in fact get much practice in talking about these things. We may think that we have faith – we are regular communicants and, if asked, we say we are Catholics. At least we may think we have the faith which is about right for where we are in the world.

At another level, there may be uncertainty, a knowing that we are only lukewarm. We may know that our faith is not strong, like the faith of saints or others we have read about. We may feel a real diffidence and incompetence about taking on the preparation of a child.

Here we need confidence at the simple psychological level, just like the confidence we have in reaching down to pick up a small child that runs towards us with its arms up ready. The child does not need or want any soul-searching or spiritual dither. It just wants easy assurance. What we are putting to the child in preparing it for first Holy Communion is as natural to it as that hug.

In his Sermon on the Mount, Jesus teaches us that sensing we are poor in spirit, is the situation of real faith. Feelings of inadequacy at least give us the assurance that we are dealing with the real issue and not just faith as a label.

Faith remains the challenge. How do we reply to the gift of faith? 'The Mass is the source and summit of the Christian life' (Catechism, 1324; *Lumen Gentium*, 11). We cannot exhaust this source, nor achieve the summit of ourselves. All is given; and in giving to the children what we have been given, we accept the mystery of these gifts and the way they make their effect in our lives. The rest we can safely entrust to Jesus, to God and his Word, to the teaching and support, through the Holy Spirit, of his Church.

The Old Testament

Background Note

The Old Testament is the story of the world as understood and told by the people of Israel. It is the story of their nation and of their changing, deepening relationship with God. It is our story too as it is the history into which Jesus, true God and true Man, was born. We belong to the New Israel, the Church of God which Jesus founded in his commission to Peter.

Who or what is God? God for the Jews is a person, Yahweh,* one person who has a relationship with his created people. The ancient account of this relationship begins with the story of how God made the world and the first people, Adam and Eve. God gave Adam and Eve free will, the power to choose, and told them not to eat of the fruit of the tree of knowledge. If they did eat this fruit, they would know the difference between good and evil. They would die. Tempted by the serpent 'to be as gods', they eat the fruit and God sends them out of the garden, doomed to live a life of toil and hardship.

---

* Yahweh is the name which God reveals to Moses (Exodus 3:13–15) and represents God's saying to Moses 'I am he who is'. Yahweh is the God of the Covenant and this name is frequently retained in the translations of the Old Testament.

The Old Testament tells how this disobedience spreads throughout the world and how God finally, according to the story, in exasperation sends a flood to destroy the evil. He spares Noah who takes two of every animal into the ark to survive the waters. After this the first fathers and great leaders of Israel come into the story. Abraham, who lived about 1,850 years before Christ, was a descendant of Noah and the first great leader of the people of Israel. He lived in the desert with his tribe and his flocks. God promises him a land for his people, a land of milk and honey, a release from the harsh existence of the nomad. Abraham leads his people to the land promised him by God.

The people are then led by Abraham's son, Isaac, and by his son, Jacob. About one hundred and fifty years later, Joseph leads them into Egypt. At first, the Jews are successful in Egypt, but then they begin to suffer. About 1,250 years before Christ, God warns their leader, Moses, to lead them out of Egypt and into the desert of Sinai to escape from the cruelty of the Pharaoh. There God comes to their rescue and makes a covenant with the people, giving them laws by which they are to live. Slowly they return to the Promised Land and create kingdoms. The Old Testament contains the books of their history and of the laws by which they lived. It records the building of the temple in Jerusalem where they worshipped God.

In 587 BC, Nebuchadnezzar, the Babylonian king, besieges and destroys Jerusalem and the Israelites are transported to Babylon in Iraq. They are allowed to return some fifty years later from this exile.

After about two hundred years, Palestine was overrun by the Greeks and ruled by Alexander the Great. His descendants ruled for a hundred and fifty years and more. For a short period, priest kings freed the land from Greek rule, but they in turn were defeated by the new power from the West, the Romans who invaded in 63 BC.

The books of the Old Testament set this narrative in the more important drama of how the people of Israel could save themselves in the eyes of God; how they could make up for their mistakes and wrongdoings; and how God continually intervenes to show them how to lead better lives. The image of God is theirs, but it deepens and develops as, in great hardship and suffering, they learn.

There are the books of the holy men whom God called to announce his will to the people. These prophets describe God's true nature and his design for his world. There are also books of poetry and prayer, the Psalms, hymns of thanksgiving and of entreaty for God's help. There are books of wisdom in which are collected the secrets of life and happiness.

The religion of Israel laid great emphasis on the importance of living by the divine law, on living virtuously until the coming of the Messiah, the mysterious chosen and anointed one of God who would come to liberate the people from their sin and from their oppressors. This, we believe, is Jesus Christ who came into the world to teach us what we now believe and who died to give us eternal life.

The Old Testament authors wrote before 'God became man and dwelt amongst us'. As followers of Jesus, we read the Old Testament in the light of his teaching and the teaching of his Church. There is no incompatibility in accepting the Old Testament as the revealed word of God and yet reading it with a critical eye, informed by the teaching of Jesus. Thus we need to interpret some of the images of God presented to us in the Old Testament. These are the projections and searchings of his people – inspired, but nonetheless human, attempts to describe the mystery of God and God's will for the world. For this reason, the Old Testament has a particular attraction for the adult mind. It is human. The authors of the Old Testament were people like us and struggled with their own human desires about the kind of God they would like to have, a God, perhaps, whose power would be sympathetic to me and 'smiteful' to those unsympathetic to me.

As we read the Old Testament, the deepening understanding of God's own self and his nature which the Old Testament records, helps us to reorder our own thinking about God and prepares us to receive his own teaching in the Gospel of Jesus.

1

The Sacrifice of Communion

Cain and Abel

Genesis 4: 1–8

4:1   . . . (And Eve) gave birth to Cain. 'I have acquired a man with the help of Yahweh' she said.

4:2   She gave birth to a second child, Abel, the brother of Cain. Now Abel became a shepherd and kept flocks, while Cain tilled the soil.

4:3   Time passed and Cain brought some of the produce of the soil as an offering for Yahweh,

4:4   while Abel for his part brought the first-born of his flock and some of their fat as well. Yahweh looked with favour on Abel and his offering.

4:5   But he did not look with favour on Cain and his offering, and Cain was very angry and downcast.

4:6   Yahweh asked Cain, 'Why are you angry and downcast?

4:7   'If you are well disposed, ought you not to lift up your head? But if you are ill disposed, is not sin at the door like a crouching beast hungering for you, which you must master?'

4:8   Cain said to his brother Abel, 'Let us go out'; and

while they were in the open country, Cain set on his brother Abel and killed him.

This early passage describes the first sacrifice which man made to God. Sacrifice is a fundamental theme for our understanding of the Mass because we speak of the Mass itself as a sacrifice.

Sacrifice is an ancient practice found in the prehistory of nearly all societies and it is still a primal instinct in each of us. But it is by no means easy for us to speak of it, especially in its ritual forms. We have long lost the practice of ancient sacrifice – killing animals and burning food and even people. It is difficult to reach out for what those distant people meant by their sacrifice. What were the emotions and intentions which led people to do these things? Our attention is held in the foreground by the appearances, the strange ritual. But those sacrifices were an expression of deep attitudes and deep hopes, and these remain in our human psyche. How important it is, in looking at the figures in the Old Testament, to recognise behind these archetypal roles three-dimensional human beings, to see people to whom we may relate, whose stories can have immediate impact for you and for me. Unless we do encounter them as people, we edit out much of what they may have to say to us. We may miss the insights into the supernatural which they were inspired to give us.

We use the word 'sacrifice' to express some act of self-denial out of love of a person or some ideal. Before the prophets or any religion which we can recognise today, scholars tell us that the primary aspiration in the ritual of a sacrifice was communion, the communion which our remote ancestors believed was the right state of affairs in the community of creation. Their idea of community extended outwards from the self to include family, then clan members and tribe, then also the domestic animals on whom their lives depended, and finally the spirit beings, gods, who looked after them. All were integrated and immediate

11

members of a single community, though structured in different orders of being. Communion represented the sense of fulfilment in belonging, in being in a state of unitive relationship with that community.

Sacrifice was the ritual assertion of that communion and doubtless individuals shared in the ritual with reactions which ranged from a shallow symbolic summoning of a sense of order and security, to a deeper spiritual perception of some greater design, a divine intention towards the good, an inner reality manifested now in their communion act. This inner reality of communion was not conjured up by the ritual, but recognised and affirmed in its transcending truth by the ritual of turning in faith and belief towards it.

This sacrificial ritual was centred on the basic necessity for life: the presentation of a meal and the eating of it: a work for others and the participation in the fruits of others' work, be they creatures or gods – the process of living and of sustaining life itself.

Some suggest that in the earliest stages of society the animals were the common property of the group and that domestic animals were only killed on sacrificial occasions to be eaten. For the rest, the domestic animals were providers of milk, wool or hair, transport, and when they died, skins. We can still find traces of these attitudes to livestock and communion meals among the nomads of the Middle East. Until recent times, the bedouin could survive for months at a go on a diet of dates and their camels' milk. And even today, certainly in Arab nomadic culture, the guest not only has a right to food as a new and accepted entrant to the community, but, through sharing in food, he gains the absolute right to the group's protection, if necessary at the cost of his host's own life. Furthermore, when livestock is killed for a meal, the name of God is still uttered over it as a sacrificial ritual and without this the meat may not be eaten. The sense of community in these Semitic societies, all the stronger the further we go back in time, and always in need of repair and reaffirmation, found a sacred expression in the sacrifice of communion and its traces are still potent today.

Sacrifice as an act of thanksgiving to the gods, of petition, of reparation for sin, appears to have developed later. In earliest sacrificial communion meals, the share for the gods was burnt. This made it inalienably theirs – in their invisible sphere, not ours, and thus holy. The people ate their own share. Some later rituals provided only for the gods: the utter giving away of the victim through burning or putting aside, with the pouring away of the blood, that great symbol of life, on places or cairns which were reserved, or believed to be, for the gods alone – a transfer from hearth to altar. Here the mood of this earliest sacrificial scene from Genesis somehow suggests an occasion when Cain and Abel were not going to get a meal out of the proceedings.

A striking aspect of this passage is the way in which it describes a **God** who **is immediately present in the lives of the people.** He is part of the way they live. **Yet there is a problem.** Since Adam and Eve have had to leave the Garden of Eden following their disobedience, there is a difficulty with God, an unquietness of conscience, **a sense that the easy and loving companionship of God has been lost.** That is how it feels to them. They express it the other way about, in terms of God being angry, not in terms of their own straying from his friendship. It is a very human interpretation: the voices of the Old Testament are at once inspired and also human. **For ourselves we need always to remember** that **God is Love.** As we grow in understanding of this truth, we find how much we ourselves have been changing and growing – not God. **Neither God nor his love changes.**

After Adam and Eve leave the Garden of Eden, they have children, Cain and Abel. Cain and Abel become farmers and, wanting to please God, they offer him the first yields of their flocks and harvest. At its simplest, **the sacrifices Cain and Abel make are acts of generosity**: responding to the generosity of God in creating the livestock and crops, by **giving back to God part of their own share** of these good things. Thus Cain and Abel are going without, denying themselves what it would otherwise be quite right and proper that they should enjoy.

At another level, Cain and Abel are also giving to God their work in tending the stock and growing the crops. In that sense **they are also making an offering of themselves.** This is what we do at the offertory in presenting 'fruit of the soil and work of human hands'.

St Augustine helped our Christian understanding of sacrifice by dwelling on the meaning of the Latin word *sacrificere* – to make holy. The sacrificial offering is made holy when it is transferred from our own realm of existence to that which is divine. Holy and mysterious, it goes beyond this broken world and the reach of our daily imperfections and shabbiness. The making of a sacrifice with good intentions and with a good conscience or a pure heart obtains some of that holiness. In being open to God and not just to the self, there is some entering into grace. This is the primal and earliest apprehension of communion. **It is not that God needs our good actions. But by them we open the self to the God who is waiting to be allowed in. We become channels for his love and action in the world**, rather than points of resistance.

At first sight, the way God replies to Cain's and Abel's presents may seem arbitrary. God looks with favour on Abel's offering, but not on Cain's. We read deeper and see that God sees into Cain's anger and his mood. Was Cain cross because he did not want to take part in the sacrifice, or because he felt God had not taken enough notice of what he had brought? We do not know. God does, but does not say. He addresses Cain's conscience and uses the wonderful image of sin like a beast (other translations have 'wolf') 'crouching at the door' of Cain's soul, hungry to eat him. God encourages Cain by saying that he can conquer sin, if he really wants to. **God offers Cain hope.** Hope, the catechism teaches us, is a theological virtue, that is a virtue we cannot have of ourselves, but is **the gift of God.** We have to co-operate with the gift through our own act of will. In moments of anger in our own lives, is not hope the last thing we feel, and therefore what we most need? Anger is the passion of our threatened pride; hope the turning outwards to God, trusting that according to his will, all will be well. God offers Cain this help; **Cain does not make the act of will to reach out of himself and accept it.**

Cain is angry and going away with his brother, he kills him. This grave crime follows almost inevitably from the direction Cain takes in turning his back on God. This is a powerful picture of the nature of sin and its accumulative strength and we delude ourselves if we think we can make deals with sin, having the bits we want and promising not to do the rest. Its power over us is incremental. The image of the beast at the door reminds us of the reality. If, however, having turned away from God, we just turn back towards him, he assures us that we can recover because he will help us. This **reconciliation, intrinsic to the idea of communion in a broken world, is part of the heart of sacrifice: doing something for God for his own sake, not for ours. Hope is also intrinsic to sacrifice. We cannot see the result of our sacrifice. We have to believe in it. We have to hope in God's goodness.**

It is possible that Cain was angry with the whole plan to make a sacrifice. He may have thought it would be a waste. God in that case would seem to be suggesting to Cain that a sacrifice made grudgingly is of no value. It is also possible that Cain was angry because God had not 'looked with favour' on what he had brought from his farm. If that were so, Cain was thinking more about himself than about God. Perhaps he wanted God not just to be pleased with the sacrifice, but pleased with Cain. Was that the main point for Cain? And how often are we cross with people when they do not react as we want them to, particularly those we want to please? Love looks outwards towards others, not inwards on itself. If we are to understand God, we must not worry too much about ourselves, but listen to him. If we are making a true sacrifice, we do it selflessly, without regard to our own interest.

Whatever the thoughts with which Cain approached his sacrifice, his reaction to God is anger. His father, Adam, had committed the first great sin of disobedience to God. Cain now commits the second greatest sin, he turns away from love for his brother and kills him. Throughout the Bible, revelation stresses these two commandments: that **we should be obedient to God's will** and that **we should love one another.** That love is no less than the action in us of God's love for each of us and that obedience is no less than conforming to the will which wishes to impart that love.

The victim of Cain's anger, Abel, is in a sense also a sacrificial victim: he pays with his life for his cleaving to his God. Seen in this way, Abel is a 'type', an early model for the mystery of Christ and he is with us at the Mass, appearing in the Third Eucharistic prayer, 'Thy servant Abel . . . '

As we go to Mass and enter the Introductory Rite, the prayers which start the Mass, we need to be clear in our own minds about the solemnity and depth of the event in which we are taking our part. As in this first account of a sacrifice in Genesis, our own motives, our readiness to be open to what is happening, to the immediacy of God's presence in our lives, our readiness to respond to the gift of hope – these are important parts of our own preparation for what is about to happen. **We go to Mass together.** We are in community when we celebrate our communion, **the people of God in the presence of their God.**

2

The Sacrifice of Thanksgiving

Noah's Sacrifice

Genesis 8: 15–22

(After the flood waters have gone back . . .)

8:15 Then God said to Noah,

8:16 'Come out of the ark, you yourself, your wife, your sons, and your sons' wives with you.

8:17 'As for all the animals with you, all things of flesh, whether birds or animals or reptiles that crawl on the earth, bring them out with you. Let them swarm on the earth; let them be fruitful and multiply on the earth.'

8:18 So Noah went out with his sons, his wife, and his sons' wives.

8:19 And all the wild beasts, all the cattle, all the birds and all the reptiles that crawl on the earth went out from the ark, one kind after another.

8:20 Noah built an altar for Yahweh, and choosing from all the clean animals and all the clean birds he offered burnt-offerings on the altar.

8:21   Yahweh smelt the appeasing fragrance and said to himself, 'Never again will I curse the earth because of man, because his heart contrives evil from his infancy. Never again will I strike down every living thing as I have done.

8:22   'As long as earth lasts, sowing and reaping, cold and heat, summer and winter, day and night shall cease no more.'

Unknowable events! We can only imagine what events or memories, glimmerings or explanations of assumed events, caused this unshakeable tradition that there was some disaster which threatened all life on the earth, but that God saved the life we see about us now. Archaeologists speculate about various disasters which overcame the earth, or parts of it, in earliest times. Was this flood the creation of the Black Sea? Who knows? No theories can compete with this vivid account formulated those thousands of years ago.

God saves Noah because he is upright and good. The account of God's motives is human, but what is plain is the writer's recognition that we depend entirely on the mercy and goodness of God. Without God's holding us up every moment of our lives, we too must cease to exist. We can try to, but ultimately we cannot, keep ourselves alive.

Noah sees this and is quite simple and straightforward about it. **The sacrifice Noah wants to make to God**, is not in thanksgiving for the good things which God has sent him, as for Cain and Abel, but **thanksgiving for life itself**, his own and the lives of those saved in the ark. After the flood, they are all that is left on the earth. As a community they offer their thanks.

Noah's sacrifice returns to God the life of some of the animals saved. The ancient writer gives a marvellously human picture of God liking the smell of the roasting. And God

18

apparently changes his mind about humans and says he will never again send a disaster to destroy all life.

The imagery again is human but derives from a conviction born of anxiety or experience. Such disasters were evidently present in the imagination of the ancients, but the God they knew was an amenable God. He had a basic goodwill towards men. So much was this true – and so true was it that prayer and sacrifice sincerely offered could return man to God's favour – that there was hope for the future, a conviction that God who had the power to destroy, would in fact preserve.

This sacrifice of Noah's marks a high point of faith. Like his descendant Abraham, Noah is famous for his faith and his friendship with God. Across many generations, the Jews suffered the pain of feeling that their friendship with God was impaired, or broken on the hardness of their hearts. **Noah's example encouraged them** on their long spiritual journey **and he encourages us as well**.

Later God tells Noah, 'I give you everything with this exception: you must not eat flesh with life, that is to say blood, in it. And I shall demand an account of your lifeblood too' (Exodus 9:4–5). The sanctity of life is God's. The sanctity of life symbolised in blood is not our share, but must be reserved for God. In our case also, he will hold us to the enormous responsibility of our actions, the knowledge of good and evil. The theme of communion is explicitly developing also its moral dimension. **God has given us the gift of free will. There is an act of will, of choice, in being open to the friendship of God, in sharing in his community and his communion.**

3

The Sacrifice of Faith

Abraham's Sacrifice

Genesis 22: 1–18

22:1   It happened some time later that God put Abraham to
the test. 'Abraham, Abraham,' he called. 'Here I am,'
Abraham replied.

22:2   'Take your son,' God said 'your only child Isaac,
whom you love, and go to the land of Moriah. There
you shall offer him as a burnt offering, on a mountain
I will point out to you.'

22:3   Rising early next morning Abraham saddled his ass
and took with him two of his servants and his son
Isaac. He chopped wood for the burnt offering and
started on his journey to the place God had pointed
out to him.

22:4   On the third day Abraham looked up and saw the
place in the distance.

22:5   Then Abraham said to his servants, 'Stay here with the
donkey. The boy and I will go over there; we will
worship and come back to you.'

22:6   Abraham took the wood for the burnt offering, loaded
it on Isaac, and carried in his own hands the fire and
the knife. Then the two of them set out together.

22:7 Isaac spoke to his father Abraham, 'Father' he said. 'Yes, my son' he replied. 'Look,' he said 'here are the fire and the wood, but where is the lamb for the burnt offering?'

22:8 Abraham answered, 'My son, God himself will provide the lamb for the burnt offering.' Then the two of them went on together.

22:9 When they arrived at the place God had pointed out to him, Abraham built an altar there, and arranged the wood. Then he bound his son Isaac and put him on the altar on top of the wood.

22:10 Abraham stretched out his hand and seized the knife to kill his son.

22:11 But the angel of Yahweh called to him from heaven. 'Abraham, Abraham' he said. 'I am here' he replied.

22:12 'Do not raise your hand against the boy' the angel said. 'Do not harm him, for now I know you fear God. You have not refused me your son, your only son.'

22:13 Then looking up, Abraham saw a ram caught by its horns in a bush. Abraham took the ram and offered it as a burnt offering in place of his son.

22:14 Abraham called this place 'Yahweh provides', and hence the saying today: On the mountain Yahweh provides.

22:15 The angel of Yahweh called Abraham a second time from heaven.

22:16 'I swear by my own self – it is Yahweh who speaks – because you have done this, because you have not refused me your son, your only son,

22:17 'I will shower blessings on you, I will make your descendants as many as the stars of heaven and the grains of sand on the seashore. Your descendants shall gain possession of the gates of their enemies.

22:18 'All the nations of the earth shall bless themselves by your descendants, as a reward for your obedience.'

Here we have sacrifice of quite a different kind. A question lurks in the mind, 'What kind of God could do this to Abraham and to the boy?' The historical context helps. Like many tribes in early history, the Canaanites, a neighbouring tribe, were given to human sacrifice, burning their sons and daughters to their god, Molech (2 Kings 23:10). The idea was therefore by no means as strange to Abraham, as it is to us. Abraham's faith may well have been tormented on that slow journey to the mountain and he may have been at his wits' end when he reached the place pointed out to him. Nonetheless, he did not give up, did not turn away. 'Though there seemed no hope, he hoped' (Romans 4:18). **Abraham followed his conscience and did his best.**

Abraham learns something new about the vastness and mystery of the will of God and a new dimension to faith and sacrifice. The sacrifice of Abraham's faith – his self-denying obedience even in the face of the disaster of having to kill his own son – becomes a gateway through which great grace and blessings reach not just himself, but reach his people – a communion of grace achieved before the ritual is completed. Intending, like Cain and Abel, to make a sacrifice of thanksgiving to God, Abraham's sacrifice of faith becomes a participation in the Father's gift of love. **Abraham shares in God's love and passes it on to his descendants.** As the people of the New Israel which is the Church, Abraham is our Patriarch also and we, in our lives today, are also beneficiaries of this extraordinary scene. It is a narrative from an ancestral past and a remarkable evocation of the mystery of God's love present and immediate to us.

God provides the ram for Abraham to sacrifice in place of Isaac, and thus teaches Abraham about **the holiness of human life**, deepening the message given to Noah (Exodus 9: 4–5). Later in the Bible, this prohibition on the sacrifice of people is made explicit (Leviticus 20).

The emptiness of Abraham's situation is arresting. Until the angel speaks, he seems thoroughly alone in his faith. The saying, 'On the mountain God provides' well captures this experience. God ultimately is the provider, not ourselves. In another way, we sometimes only let God provide when we have exhausted our own reliance on ourselves.

St John of the Cross in the seventeenth century had another saying, 'On the mountain nothing'. The ascent up the mountain represents our spiritual journey closer to God. At the top there is no 'I've made it', no grand climax of fulfilment in terms which we might want or understand earlier in the journey. There is simply God, as for Abraham, greater and more mysterious than we had ever thought. He provides what, in his infinite wisdom and love for us, he knows we need. **It does not matter whether we can see the good we do, the blessings which sacrifices can bring to others. It does not matter whether we can feel** in any conscious way, **the love God has for us.** 'Since it belongs to the supernatural order, *grace escapes our experience* and cannot be known except by faith' (Catechism, 2005). The drama of this scene expresses this truth. God replies to Abraham's action of faith and hope (though Abraham is not called upon actually to put Isaac to death – it seems his obedience is evidence enough of his faith) by pouring out blessings for his heirs and successors. Abraham cannot have known this of himself. It is the angel who tells him. It is our faith that in the sacraments we are united with those same blessings, with God's unceasing love for us.

For Abraham God comes first. The faith to let him come first in our lives is something we have to pray for. We cannot manage it by ourselves. Like hope, faith is given by the Father. It helps us not to count the cost, but to make in true love our sacrifices without thought for the return they may bring.

Love is God's greatest gift to us; we are closest to God in loving others. In sacrificial situations, God is closest to us. God's love for us does not hesitate even

23

in the face of the Passion of Jesus. We look forward to that event in this account of Abraham. He came near to having to understand the love of the Father who would not deny his own nature of love, even at the cost of the Passion, the sacrifice of faith of his Son. The Mass is the sacramental manifestation of this love which Jesus shares and has for us. When we participate in the Mass, we share in the blessings and grace which the sacrifice of Jesus, the true God and true Man, brings down on his people.

4

The Sacrifice of Salvation

The Passover

Exodus 12: 1–14

12:1 Yahweh said to Moses and Aaron in the land of Egypt,

12:2 'This month is to be the first of all the others for you, the first month of your year.

12:3 'Speak to the whole community of Israel and say, "On the tenth day of this month each man must take an animal from the flock, one for each family: one animal for each household.

12:4 "If the household is too small to eat the animal, a man must join with his neighbour, the nearest to his house, as the number of persons requires. You must take into account what each can eat in deciding the number for the animal.

12:5 "It must be an animal without blemish, a male one year old; you may take it from either sheep or goats.

12:6 "You must keep it till the fourteenth day of the month when the whole assembly of the community of Israel shall slaughter it between the two evenings.

12:7 "Some of the blood must then be taken and put on the two doorposts and the lintel of the houses where it is eaten.

12:8 "That night, the flesh is to be eaten, roasted over the fire; it must be eaten with unleavened bread and bitter herbs.

12:9 "Do not eat any of it raw or boiled, but roasted over the fire, head, feet and entrails.

12:10 "You must not leave any over till the morning: whatever is left till morning you are to burn.

12:11 "You shall eat it like this: with a girdle round your waist, sandals on your feet, a staff in your hand. You shall eat it hastily: it is a Passover in honour of Yahweh.

12:12 "That night, I will go through the land of Egypt and strike down all the first-born in the land of Egypt, man and beast alike, and I shall deal out punishment to all the gods of Egypt, I am Yahweh!

12:13 "The blood shall serve to mark the houses that you live in. When I see the blood I will pass over you and you shall escape the destroying plague when I strike the land of Egypt.

12:14 "This day is to be a day of remembrance for you, and you must celebrate it as a feast in Yahweh's honour. For all generations you are to declare it a day of festival, for ever."

After their sufferings in Egypt at the hands of the Pharaoh, God saves the people of Israel by telling Moses how they may escape. They had asked the Pharaoh for permission to celebrate a religious feast and God tells Moses that each house is to make a sacrifice in the evening, smearing blood on the doors of the houses. This will be a sign to God, as his angel passes through the country striking down all the first-born with plague, that these are the houses of his own people who are to be spared.

The people are to eat the sacrificed animals, dressed and ready for their journey. Early the next day they must leave. God leads Moses to a place where they can cross the sea into Sinai and thus escape from Egypt. Egyptian troops are sent to recapture them. The waters which had parted to allow the people through safely, close again on the Egyptians and kill them. The people of Israel make good their escape.

In this event, **through their sacrifice, God's people are spared and led out to a new life.** Their sacrifice is a communion meal: they participate in the holiness of grace through eating the burnt victim. It is also a preparation for their journey to safety. God tells them to keep this day holy as a feast day for ever after. It remains a major feast in the Jewish calendar.

God is teaching the people about themselves, who they are, how they are to keep this identity in the future through faithfulness to their relationship with God and through his feast days. The identity is not just individual, the relationship with God is not just individual. **We know who we are also through reference to those around us. Our relationship with God is also importantly expressed through our relations with those around us.** The relationship has to be lived, not just treated as an accessory, or part-time aspect of our programme.

The sacrificial meal and rite which God teaches his people are to be the sign and affirmation of this identity. **The sacrifice** does not secure their salvation in the sense that God is suggesting he would refuse to save them unless they make the sacrifice. It is not a contract. It **is his people's opportunity to know that God in his love intends to save them.** They must turn to God and self-consciously accept what he wants for them. The people are free to choose, just as Adam was free to choose to eat that apple. The Passover sacrifice, like Abraham's sacrifice, brings the people blessing from God: deliverance from Egypt, and the start of a new life.

There is a rite in the sacrifice as there is in the Mass. God's instructions are precise. The holy sacrifice, like the identity, is not an individual matter, but for, with and by the people. The right thing is to be done in the right way, formally, ritually. It transcends personality, the ego with its likes and dislikes. Holiness is greater than this. People are called, in the end, to a perfection of living in God's love. It may, as Abraham and St John of the Cross found, feel like nothing. The Mass may feel like nothing. This simply emotional response does not matter. The formality of the ritual gives us the opportunity to choose to do the right thing properly and faith leaves us open to the action of God which is promised us.

The communion meal is also a preparation for the journey to safety: an outward sign of what is happening to them, not only in the drama of their escape, but also in their interior relationship with God. The old catechism defined **a sacrament** as **an outward sign of an inward grace** and this Passover meal provides an example of this dual action. **At the sacrament of the Mass we take food**, although in only a symbolic amount, **which feeds us** materially and **in the spirit.** We are sustained in our journey through life and also spiritually protected by grace, just as the Israelites were physically protected from the fate of the Egyptians. Moses can be seen as an early type, or prefiguring, of the person of Jesus. **Jesus instituted the Mass at the Last Supper at Passover time. His own death was a sacrifice in that he accepted it freely. His resurrection began a new life for us.**

5

Food for the Journey

The Manna

Exodus 16: 1–15

16:1 From Elim they set out again, and the whole community of the sons of Israel reached the wilderness of Sin – between Elim and Sinai – on the fifteenth day of the second month after they had left Egypt.

16:2 And the whole community of the sons of Israel began to complain against Moses and Aaron in the wilderness

16:3 and said to them, 'Why did we not die at Yahweh's hand in the land of Egypt, when we were able to sit down to pans of meat and could eat bread to our heart's content? As it is, you have brought us to this wilderness to starve this whole company to death!'

16:4 Then Yahweh said to Moses, 'Now I will rain down bread for you from the heavens. Each day the people are to go out and gather the day's portion; I propose to test them in this way to see whether they will follow my law or not.

16:5 'On the sixth day, when they prepare what they have brought in, this will be twice as much as the daily gathering.'

16:6 Moses and Aaron said to the whole community of the sons of Israel, 'In the evening you shall learn that it was Yahweh who brought you out of the land of Egypt,

16:7 'and in the morning you shall see the glory of Yahweh, for he has heard your complaints against him – it is not against us you complain, for what are we?'

16:8 Moses said, 'In the evening Yahweh will give you meat to eat, in the morning bread to your heart's content, for Yahweh has heard the complaints you made against him; your complaining is not against us – for what are we? – but against Yahweh.'

16:9 Moses said to Aaron, 'To the whole community of the sons of Israel say this, "Present yourselves before Yahweh, for he has heard your complaints".'

16:10 As Aaron was speaking to the whole community of the sons of Israel, they turned towards the wilderness, and there was the glory of Yahweh appearing in the form of a cloud.

16:11 Then Yahweh spoke to Moses and said,

16:12 'I have heard the complaints of the sons of Israel. Say this to them, "Between the two evenings you shall eat meat, and in the morning you shall have bread to your heart's content. Then you will learn that I, Yahweh, am your God".'

16:13 And so it came about: quails flew up in the evening, and they covered the camp; in the morning there was a coating of dew all round the camp.

16:14 When the coating of dew lifted, there on the surface of the desert was a thing delicate, powdery, as fine as hoarfrost on the ground.

16:15 When they saw this, the sons of Israel said to one another, 'What is that?' not knowing what it was. 'That' said Moses to them 'is the bread Yahweh gives you to eat.'

Struggling across the empty desert, the Israelites are hungry, depressed and afraid. They can see no escape from the new dangers they face: getting lost in the desert and starvation. They begin to quarrel with Moses, saying that they would have been better off, if they had stayed in Egypt. At least in Egypt they had plenty to eat and drink.

The people are beginning to lose the faith in God which had helped them to escape. In spite of all this, God now intervenes to give them another chance. He tells Moses that he will send miraculous bread down from heaven to feed them. They will still have to keep his law by not working on the Sabbath – the seventh day on which God himself rested after creating the world. They must therefore collect enough of the miraculous bread on the sixth day to last them through the seventh.

Moses explains this to the people and says that the bread and the meat of the quails will prove to them that it was God who saved them, and not some idea of his own. The people's complaints are against God and not against Moses or his brother Aaron.

While Aaron is explaining all this to the people, they see in the clouds over the desert the glory of God. God tells Moses that he has heard the complaints of his people. He will help them. He knows that his people are weak, but he is full of mercy. The arrival of the quails provided meat in plenty, and the Manna found on the desert floor in the early morning tasted like honeyed wafers. **The Manna kept them going on their journey to a new life in the promised land.**

It is exciting to imagine this scene. Even today, large numbers of quail arrive on the coast of the Sinai peninsula migrating south from Europe after the summer. They arrive exhausted and are not that difficult to catch. Was the Israelites' journey also in the autumn? After the long desert summer, the autumn evenings can be dramatic with huge clouds building up in the sky, shot through with the light and colour of sunset. Perhaps in such circumstances, the people see the glory of

God. **They are not alone in their troubles. Neither ever are we.**

God is present at all times. We can think we catch sight of his glory in the beauty and solitude of nature. Whether we do, or not, he is always in our 'here'. In putting ourselves into this scene in Sinai, does the scene not also quickly rehearse itself in our own lives here? We can recall our own moments of despair and fear.

God touches again on ritual in his instructions about not collecting the food from the desert on the seventh day. Ritual only has vitality as an attempt to do something important in the right way, especially when we are upset and not feeling organised.

'As a social animal, man is a ritual animal.'★ Our individuality and individualism reveal our personal weakness and vulnerability. Custom and ritual enable us to express what perhaps we cannot articulate for ourselves. Ritual provides not only idiom for our deepest thoughts, but also a protective cipher for what we might otherwise fear or be too shy to express, or say that we want to learn. For ritual also provides access to new knowledge. It has not only an instrumental efficacy, but another kind also 'achieved in the action itself, in the assertion it makes and the experience which bears its imprinting.'★★ The plain danger of ritual is that it can become empty of commitment, simply a matter of conformity. The same danger is present in our attitude to the law, God's law, and to the Mass.

★ Mary Douglas (1996) *Purity and Danger*, Routledge, London, Ark Paperback edition, p. 63.
★★ Ibid., p. 69.

The Israelites may have been tempted to think of the law as prohibitions. Another way of looking at law is to see an opportunity to do things rightly. This requires will power. Our will power is constantly being tested and refined in our own lives. We need this if we are to conform our will to that of the Father, wanting what he wants.

In our own minds, it may be helpful to reflect that, in theology, the will is linked with the theological virtue of hope (cf. Cain) and that of faith is linked with the mind. Hope helps the will and faith helps the mind and our use of will and mind helps open us to faith and hope.

6

The Covenant of Love: Life in Freedom

The Ten Commandments

Exodus 19: 3–8

19:3   Moses then went up to God, and Yahweh called to him from the mountain, saying 'Say this to the House of Jacob, declare this to the sons of Israel,

19:4   "You yourselves have seen what I did with the Egyptians, how I carried you on eagle's wings and brought you to myself.

19:5   "From this you know that now, if you obey my voice and hold fast to my covenant, you of all the nations shall be my very own for all the earth is mine.

19:6   "I will count you a kingdom of priests, a consecrated nation." Those are the words you are to speak to the sons of Israel.'

19:7   So Moses went and summoned the elders of the people, putting before them all that Yahweh had bidden him.

19:8   Then all the people answered as one, 'All that Yahweh has said, we will do.' And Moses took the people's reply back to Yahweh.

A covenant is more than an agreement, it is a bond, a binding undertaking. God's promise to the people of Israel as they journey away from Egypt into the East, is that he will make them 'a holy nation'. God's bond, from his side, is unconditional. To take their share of what God is offering them, the people must obey his commandments. The people are enthusiastic about this offer and Moses leads them to the foot of the mountain where God will announce to him the commandments which they are to keep.

God's purpose and desire for his people is that they should share in his life, that in communion they should enjoy the intimate security of his friendship, as at first had Adam and Eve in the Garden of Eden. God's desire is not changed. The bond, the covenant, he offers Moses seems for the people the tentative beginning of a path back to that union with the life of God. In these commandments, God tells his people how they are to lead their lives in order to receive all that he wants to give them. As Christians, we look forward here to the deathless covenant, the union of God with humanity, which we receive in Jesus and which at Mass is brought to each of us in eternal immediacy.

Moses goes up the mountain which is covered with smoke and fire, and God gives him the Ten Commandments:

Extracted from Exodus 20: 1–17

20:1 Then God spoke all these words. He said,

20:2 'I am Yahweh your God who brought you out of the land of Egypt, out of the house of slavery.

20:3 'You shall have no gods except me.

20:4 'You shall not make yourself a carved image or any likeness of anything in heaven or on earth beneath or in the waters under the earth;

20:5 'you shall not bow down to them or serve them. For I, Yahweh your God, am a jealous God and I punish the father's fault in the sons, the grandsons, and the great-grandsons of those who hate me;

20:6 'but I show kindness to thousands of those who love me and keep my commandments.

20:7 'You shall not utter the name of Yahweh your God to misuse it, for Yahweh will not leave unpunished the man who utters his name to misuse it.

20:8 'Remember the sabbath day and keep it holy.

20:9 'For six days you shall labour and do all your work,

20:10 'but the seventh day is a sabbath for Yahweh your God. You shall do no work that day, neither you nor your son nor your daughter nor your servants, men or women, nor your animals nor the stranger who lives with you.

20:11 'For in six days Yahweh made the heavens and the earth and the sea and all that these hold, but on the seventh day he rested; that is why Yahweh has blessed the sabbath day and made it sacred.

20:12 'Honour your father and your mother so that you may have a long life in the land that Yahweh your God has given to you.

20:13 'You shall not kill.

20:14 'You shall not commit adultery.

20:15 'You shall not steal.

20:16 'You shall not bear false witness against your neighbour.

20:17 'You shall not covet your neighbour's house. You shall not covet your neighbour's wife, or his servant, man or woman, or his ox, or his donkey, or anything that is his.'

God is all-powerful and he is present in our lives. In the first commandment, God contrasts himself with our own idols – the projections of our imagination. And how often in fact is this idolatry the underlying assumption of our own dealings with God? The promises we make in a tight corner, 'Get me out of this, Lord, and I shall . . . ', may reveal a natural tendency to regard God as just another accessory to our experience, engaged or ignored as the mood strikes us.

Here God announces that he is himself and none other, vital and active in our lives, not an image to be picked up and put down. In the second commandment, God seems to beg us to avoid attitudes and behaviour which show our disregard for his presence. Do we not speak too freely of God in any case, never mind take his name in vain? God's Holy Name, unmentionable in Old Testament tradition – it was so holy – is an expression of the enormity of God's mystery. **At the beginning of the commandments, God makes this invitation to faith. Can we accept him on his own terms, rather than on ours?**

It is not easy for us to know what those distant Israelites made of this communication from God. Our own understanding has been deepened by the teaching of Jesus at the Last Supper, **'I give you a new commandment: love one another; you must love one another just as I have loved you. It is by your love for one another that everyone will recognise you as my disciples.'** (John 13:34–35).

God is love. This we know is the fundamental principle with which to seek an understanding of God's will. God's own attitude to us is not conditional on how we behave towards him; but our ability to receive him is to a great extent conditional on our attitude to him. Our ideas of morality should not be drawn from a starting assumption that we need to comply with a range of precepts or rules, in order to put ourselves right with God. Instead, we remember Cain who, at the level of what he did, did comply – he did bring his sacrifice. The issue was what was his motive? Did Cain love? And when Cain turned away in anger he turned to himself, in on himself, and great sin soon followed. Jesus unambiguously teaches this priority of the inner, spiritual dimension of morality in his Sermon on the Mount (Matthew 5:20–48). He shows how an action may be judged by men, but the attitude which precedes it will also be judged by God. It does the adult mind a power of good to read that passage in Matthew, when reflecting on the Ten Commandments.

Moral action is not only acting out and participating in God's own goodness, it also embraces the attitude of openness to God's covenant of unceasing love for us. This love is wonderfully described in another account of Moses and the Ten Commandments: 'Yahweh set his heart on you and chose you not because you were the most numerous of all peoples – for indeed you were the smallest of all – but because he loved you and meant to keep the oath which he swore to your ancestors . . . ' (Deuteronomy 7:7–8).

Turning to that love and being open to it, the desire to keep these ten commandments grows in us. The commandments outline the conditions, or characteristics, of the free life which the people are to enjoy after their salvation from Egypt.

If we are to collaborate with the gift of faith, we need to promote that desire for the good. Through attraction or negation? We Catholics used to be a byword for having difficulties with feelings of guilt. This is dangerous ground for parents. A presentation of religion which is prohibitive, will in the end be just that for the young: a prohibitive proposition which is not accepted in the terms put. We need a sense of the law and educated consciences. But the old analogy with light is helpful. A surface may look clean, but a brighter light will reveal dust and specks not seen before. So it is with our souls. We become more aware of our imperfections as we grow in God. But God must be our gaze, not ourselves. That sense of the law of God and moral imperatives will grow in so far as we remember, contemplate and, in the end, inescapably enact God's great love for his world.

The small part we have to play in his covenant of love will be a natural response if we give that covenant our attention.

A Jewish anecdote. When Tel Aviv was being built up early in the twentieth century, a very holy old rabbi lived in a street without street lights. The council installed a light outside his house, in honour of his service to the people. Later the old man commented that he noticed that as he came along the street at night, his shadow was long. As he approached the lamp and his door, his shadow shrank. Right under the lamp, he had almost no shadow at all and his home was at hand. He likened the lamp to the Torah, the law, and his shadow to himself.

7

Waybread for the Pilgrim

Elijah and the Angel

1 Kings 19: 3–8

19:3   ... (Elijah) came to Beersheba, a town of Judah, where he left his servant.

19:4   He himself went on into the wilderness, a day's journey, and sitting under a furze bush wished he were dead. 'Yahweh,' he said 'I have had enough. Take my life; I am no better than my ancestors.'

19:5   Then he lay down and went to sleep. But an angel touched him and said, 'Get up and eat.'

19:6   He looked round, and there at his head was a scone baked on hot stones, and a jar of water. He ate and drank and then lay down again.

19:7   But the angel of Yahweh came back a second time and touched him and said, 'Get up and eat, or the journey will be too long for you.'

19:8   So he got up and ate and drank, and strengthened by that food he walked for forty days and forty nights until he reached Horeb, the mountain of God.

The prophet Elijah lived in the Holy Land when Ahab was king of Israel. Ahab ruled 874–53 BC. He worshipped the pagan god, Baal, in defiance of the first commandment and built a temple to him. Elijah told Ahab that no rain would fall in Israel until he, Elijah, said so. Thereafter Elijah had constant problems with Ahab.

Here we find the prophet in fear of his life from the king's men, making his way to Horeb, another name for Mount Sinai, the mountain of God. He hoped like Moses to be able to speak to God and learn what he should do next.

Elijah is exhausted and cast down. Like the Israelites after their escape from Egypt, he is oppressed by his troubles and by the desert. He is not, however, sorry for himself. He commits himself to the mercy of God: he says he can of himself do no more. God sends an angel to feed him and save him. **The miraculous food strengthens him for his long journey through the desert to the place where he will meet God.**

A prophetic literal image of the Eucharist. This story is **an assurance of the help which God gives whenever we turn to him.** By the gift of faith and the deepening of our faith as life goes on, we learn to live in the confidence of that help. This means being sure of it, whether or not we can recognise this or that happening in answer to our prayers.

Sharing in the Eucharist at Mass is a principal way of deepening our faith as the Mass is a very perfect form of prayer. The Catechism describes it as 'The summit and source of the Christian life' (Catechism, 1324). The waybread we receive (and such is its name when given to the dying) is the body of Christ and, whether or not we can perceive its effects at the time, it strengthens us in faith and for our journey to our own meeting with God.

8

God's Secrecy in His Sacraments

Isaiah Prophesies the Coming of Immanuel: Three Readings

Isaiah 7: 14–15

7:14   The Lord himself, therefore, will give you a sign. It is this: the maiden is with child and will soon give birth to a son whom she will call Immanuel.

7:15   On curds and honey will he feed until he knows how to refuse evil and choose good.

Isaiah 9: 5–6

9:5   For there is a child born for us, a son given to us and dominion is laid on his shoulders; and this is the name they give him: Wonder-Counsellor, Mighty-God, Eternal-Father, Prince-of-Peace.

9:6   Wide is his dominion in a peace that has no end, for the throne of David and for his royal power, which he establishes and makes secure in justice and integrity. From this time onwards and for ever, the jealous love of Yahweh Sabaoth will do this.

Isaiah 11: 1–9

11:1   A shoot springs from the stock of Jesse, a scion thrusts from his roots:

11:2   on him the spirit of Yahweh rests, a spirit of wisdom and insight, a spirit of counsel and power, a spirit of knowledge and of the fear of Yahweh. (The fear of Yahweh is his breath.)

11:3   He does not judge by appearances, he gives no verdict on hearsay,

11:4   but judges the wretched with integrity, and with equity gives a verdict for the poor of the land. His word is a rod that strikes the ruthless, his sentences bring death to the wicked.

11:5   Integrity is the loincloth round his waist, faithfulness the belt about his hips.

11:6   The wolf lives with the lamb, the panther lies down with the kid, calf and lion cub feed together with a little boy to lead them.

11:7   The cow and the bear make friends, their young lie down together. The lion eats straw like the ox.

11:8   The infant plays over the cobra's hole; into the viper's lair the young child puts his hand.

11:9   They do no hurt, no harm, on all my holy mountain, for the country is filled with the knowledge of Yahweh as the waters swell the sea.

The prophet Isaiah was born about 765 BC and these three short passages were written sometime after 740 BC. **They prophesy the coming of the Messiah** – the anointed one of God. **Immanuel means 'God is with us'.** Jesse was the father of David, the great king of Israel. **Joseph, Mary's husband and kinsman, was descended from David's line** (Matthew 1:1).

These passages well illustrate the mystery of prophecy. We tend to think of the prophet as one who foretells the future and today we can quickly say that we can see how these statements of Isaiah's look forward to the incarnation and to the role of Mary. But what a depth and density of meaning lie beyond that quick assessment. How obscure and inscrutable these words must have appeared to those who pondered them over the intervening seven centuries. Even during and after the life of Christ many will have toyed with these ancient echoes and still been unsure what to make of the associations which they evoked.

Are we really any surer today? The appearance of 'God with us' in the form of a baby and the proclamation of wide dominion and peace – these are extraordinary notions to set beside our usual ideas of God and our usual experience of the world. While assenting to the facts, we can remain prisoners of habit at one level though, at another, restless. We disengage from meanings which seem familiar and therefore do not speak particularly to us where we are now. Those meanings, perhaps first lodged in haste and in very early years, scarcely revisited since, need a new reflection. We have a tendency to reduce God; and this is proportionate to our tendency not to learn about him. Christians have no other way to God but Christ. 'I am the way . . . ' (John 14:6). We need to return to his Word in revelation with new eyes, new ears.

To prophesy, in its first meaning, means to speak out the will of God. Of course, stared at, the will of God is inscrutable. But it does reveal itself in retrospect in so far as we make an effort to conform to it. It does reveal itself in answer to reflection and prayer, even though in hidden ways which are dark until later experience and faith illuminate them.

Moses' experience sharply reminds us of this. When God is near him on the mountain, God tells him to hide in a cleft in the rock where he will also cover him with his hand, for 'No man shall see my face and live', but 'the glory of my passing you shall see' (Exodus 33:23). And so is our experience of God's action in our own lives. It can only be seen in retrospect. If we can see that this is so, we are on the way to accepting that his action is there, active and attentive, even though at the time we do not notice it. This secrecy of God is present in the sacraments and in our living in them.

9

The Silent Prayer of the Contrite Heart

Further Thoughts on Sacrifice

Psalm 40: 5–8

40:5 How many wonders you have done for us, Yahweh, my God! How many plans you have made for us; you have no equal! I want to proclaim them, again and again, but they are more than I can count.

40:6 You, who wanted no sacrifice or oblation, opened my ear, you asked no holocaust or sacrifice for sin;

40:7 then I said, 'Here I am! I am coming!' In the scroll of the book am I not commanded

40:8 to obey your will? My God, I have always loved your Law from the depths of my being.

Psalm 51: 14–17

51:14 Save me from death, God my saviour, and my tongue will acclaim your righteousness;

51:15 Lord, open my lips, and my mouth will speak out your praise.

51:16 Sacrifice gives you no pleasure, were I to offer holocaust, you would not have it.

51:17 My sacrifice is this broken spirit, you will not scorn this crushed and broken heart.

These two passages from the Psalms probably date from the reign of David who ruled 1010–970 BC. A new note has entered the language of worship and sacrifice. The authors of these lines know of a God who may be addressed directly, but they know he surpasses human understanding. They see his glory in what he has done for them, his power in what they know he may do. **Before such a God they want to say much. At the same time they are without words – simply 'I am coming', 'Open my lips', 'A broken spirit'.** These are wonderful glimpses into prayer: the talkative self moving into the silence of the closeness of God.

These prayerful writers are reflecting on the danger that acts of worship and sacrifice can lose their sincerity and meaning without the motive of love. If the rite becomes empty ritual, then its value is lost. They perceive that God cannot be fobbed off with sacrifice despatched like a tax return. God in himself has no need of the victims. **Contact with God, a person in relationship with those he loves, happens in his own medium of love: the offering, surrendering of the soul.**

The first passage beautifully **expresses the love of God into which we hope to grow. God gives him the grace of 'an open ear', the faith to attend on God.** This response is simply to want to be closer to God. This being closer may in practice be learning, reading more about God and, in so doing, trying to live closer to God's will through good and sensitive behaviour towards others. Inside, imperceptibly to the mind and emotion, the soul is also moving closer to its Creator. Once that outward, searching movement of the soul is begun, the soul, in St John of the Cross's beautiful phrase, 'knows its true place and strives to reach it'.

The second passage sees the snares of self-importance and self-satisfaction in religious observance. Were the priests and people rather pleased with how well they were making their sacrifices? Were they concentrating too much on their own participation in holiness? The author of this psalm knows that **before God's inexpressible goodness, the human soul is humble.** If it knows of that goodness, it is humble. The goodness of God leaves no space for self-importance. But we all are self-important: we each matter very much to ourselves. And looking into the goodness of God, we know how true this is and we know in turn 'the broken spirit, the contrite heart'. It is in ourselves. This is not a source of shame or resentment. As this psalm assures us, God is not one to scorn such a person: instead, his love can reach a heart not caught up with itself, not locked in by the choices of the free will God's love has given us. Don't we need to lay aside our misapprehensions about some clash of wills, try to lie open to the mind of the Father, secure in the faith that his mind is unconditional and absolute love?

These psalms open for us a further understanding of Jesus' humble acceptance of, his preference for, the will of the Father. They lead us towards the sacrifice of Jesus: the paschal, or Passover, mystery which we sense through our very earliest instincts about the need for sacrifice and its value. When sacrifice is symbolic it needs ritual to be effective. The sacrifice of the self is not symbolic and its drama transcends ritual.

10

The Mystery of Suffering:
Sacrifice and Expiation

The Mysterious Servant in Isaiah

Isaiah 52: 13–15 and 53: 1–12

52:13 See, my servant will prosper, he shall be lifted up, exalted, rise to great heights.

52:14 As the crowds were appalled on seeing him – so disfigured did he look that he seemed no longer human –

52:15 so will the crowds be astonished at him, and kings stand speechless before him; for they shall see something never told and witness something never heard before.

53:1 'Who could believe what we have heard, and to whom has the power of Yahweh been revealed?'

53:2 Like a sapling he grew up in front of us, like a root in arid ground. Without beauty, without majesty (we saw him), no looks to attract our eyes;

53:3 a thing despised and rejected by men, a man of sorrows and familiar with suffering, a man to make people screen their faces; he was despised and we took no account of him.

53:4 And yet ours were the sufferings he bore, ours the sorrows he carried. But we, we thought of him as someone punished, struck by God, and brought low.

53:5 Yet he was pierced through for our faults, crushed for our sins. On him lies a punishment that brings us peace, and through his wounds we are healed.

53:6 We had all gone astray like sheep, each taking his own way, and Yahweh burdened him with the sins of all of us.

53:7 Harshly dealt with, he bore it humbly, he never opened his mouth, like a lamb that is led to the slaughter-house, like a sheep that is dumb before its shearers never opening its mouth.

53:8 By force and by law he was taken; would anyone plead his cause? Yes, he was torn away from the land of the living; for our faults struck down in death.

53:9 They gave him a grave with the wicked, a tomb with the rich, though he had done no wrong and there had been no perjury in his mouth.

53:10 Yahweh has been pleased to crush him with suffering. If he offers his life in atonement, he shall see his heirs, he shall have a long life and through him what Yahweh wishes will be done.

53:11 His soul's anguish over he shall see the light and be content. By his sufferings shall my servant justify many, taking their faults on himself.

53:12 Hence I will grant whole hordes for his tribute, he shall divide the spoil with the mighty, for surrendering himself to death and letting himself be taken for a sinner, while he was bearing the faults of many and praying all the time for sinners.

A very difficult but important passage. These lines, with the powerful images of the sheep and 'his tomb with the rich', are strongly allusive to the fate of Jesus and his burial in the

50

tomb of Joseph of Arimathaea. They bring us face to face with the mystery of suffering. We cannot resolve the mystery of suffering and our belief in a God who passionately loves us. But we must not shirk it, put it out of mind as too difficult, or allow it to erode faith with pessimism or cynicism. We have to try to stand in its presence and endure it.

The speaker is an unknown prophet we call Second Isaiah who wrote early in the sixth century BC, about one hundred and fifty years after Isaiah, the author of the passage about Immanuel.

These lines are taken from the last of the four 'Songs of the Servant' in the book. The identity of the Servant is not disclosed, but he personifies the prophet's insight that **the man of God will suffer in this world.** God's ways are not the ways of the world. The world is concerned with itself and its powers, not with God. The petitions that God give victory to the righteous over the iniquitous, are silent. The servant will attain the light and be content, but after he has passed through death. **The true horizon of our lives** emerges. It **is eternity.**

The servant is not only a negligible, unattractive person, but he is so afflicted that we in the world avoid him. In our own lives we think of the poor and homeless in the cities whom we hurry past on the pavement.

Second Isaiah tells us that *we assume* that the servant's fate is his own due, then that in fact **the servant's fate is the consequence of our own sins.** This may shock, but it is not incomprehensible: an innocent man, he suffers at the hands of the unthinking, the uninterested, the heartless. And are we not often in effect insensitive, heartless? We participate in inflicting suffering when we are. But in some way, Second Isaiah says, **the way the servant bears his affliction, frees us.**

How is this? A back reference to the Jews' rite for the Day of Atonement. The rite is described by Leviticus (Leviticus 16:21–22). Before the priest enters the Holy of Holies at the Temple (which only he may enter) to complete the sacrifice, a goat is brought forward and the priest lays his hands on its head. In doing this, he symbolically transfers to the goat the sins of the people. It is then driven out into the wilderness. In its alienation, the goat takes the sins of the city away. There are echoes of this in the event of Jesus's exorcising the demoniac at Gadara, when he casts the evil spirits into the pigs which throw themselves over the cliff.

Thus deep in the human psyche, we find the powerful, but difficult – because we do not understand how it works – idea that a sacrifice can release sins, expiate them. Here, however, the sacrifice is not of an animal, but made by a person of himself. How could such a substitution work? Can the culpability of one be resolved through the expiatory act of another? This is very difficult for our contemporary ideas of justice. We find easier the principle that each person must take responsibility for his or her misdeeds, that a wrong incurs a debt to society which must be repaid. Could we dare take such responsibility in the eyes of God?

How can we present this to the mind of a child? How can we reach behind the barriers of the legalisms in our notions of human justice, to hope to grasp the significance of what is being suggested here, and how it works?

First we are stressing at every turn the goodness and limitless love of God. We must never obscure or confuse this fundamental truth.

Secondly, we may stress that human beings are free – but our freedom includes the freedom also to sin and our natures have an intractable inclination to sin. So we are not as free as we think we are because we are not neutral in our desires. We are not innocent. But **God in his**

limitless love wants to free us from our sins, from our natural weakness and blindness in our orientation away from pure love.

The message of Second Isaiah's Servant proposes that a person can become a means for God's work in this liberation. In accepting the mystery of suffering, a person can draw closer to God; closeness and obedience to God opens in the world a channel for his love. His love is not abstract. It is that union with God which the Ten Commandments extend to us as his will for us, his invitation to us to pure freedom.

This union with his will which transmits his love outwards and towards others, is the image of Christ, the perfect channel to the world of the Father's love. This love frees people from their sins.

Thus we may understand Second Isaiah here as saying that **when a person** *will* **not abandon love, but accepts the suffering that men inflict, then this acceptance can be turned into a dynamic action of love for others. This action draws us into the medium of love in which we are freed from sin.** For it is our experience that when we are truly loved, we aspire to the good. **Love opens our eyes to the good and works in us a liberation from the burden of our sins.**

Jesus taught that 'No greater love has a man than he lay down his life for a friend' (John 15:13). Perhaps we know, or have heard of, somebody whose life was saved by a friend's death. Can we imagine how we should feel in that situation, a friend of ours is killed so that we might live?

God will not defend himself in the disputes of men. God is on the side of the victim who can make this act of self-sacrificial love. Every parent at some time or another has an inkling of this saving grace which supports us in the difficulties of family life.

53

There are echoes here of Abraham at Moriah: Abraham is ready to accept a disaster for his son, in obedience to his understanding of God. God, however, teaches Abraham that he is not required to make that sacrifice. A ram is given instead. God himself, however, will go that further step when his own Son, Jesus, is confronted with a death, not of holy sacrifice, but of cruelty. By voluntarily accepting this death, Jesus transforms it into his own sacrifice. Jesus becomes as the sheep at the sacrifice. Like the sheep here in Second Isaiah, 'He never opened his mouth.' He knows he can release humanity from its sins, through this act of love. In Jesus's resurrection we see how humanity is freed: **Love literally overcomes death.**

Second Isaiah is proclaiming a truth in this 'Song of the Servant'. It is a truth of general human application. In Jesus the incarnate Word is both sacrificial victim and, in resurrection, the assurance of the promises of Christ. Impelled by his Father's love for the world, his sacrifice proclaims that love and wins eternal life for those who seek to follow him.

The New Testament

Background Note

The four Gospels give us accounts of the life of Jesus as the four evangelists were inspired to write them. They were probably composed in the last years of the first century AD and early in the second. They are not evidential accounts of human facts of the kind we might ourselves want to write, of incidents which we had witnessed. The Gospels present a structured understanding of both the events and purpose of the incarnation, drawing from the accounts of those who saw what happened and from the writers' own convictions about what all this meant. Thus, while we find differences of detail in the four versions of the story, the understanding of the life of Christ is one. The understanding we have of God derives from the understanding of the authors of the Gospels. We believe their accounts are a revelation of Divine Truth. For Christians, objective reality − the reality which transcends the mutabilities of this broken world − is the content of this revelation.

The Acts of the Apostles and the Letters also contained in the New Testament are themselves part of this revelation and they deepen our understanding of it. The theology presented in the letters encourages us to learn what God meant by the events of the life of Jesus and to place that understanding in our own lives through our own prayer.

11

The Inscrutability of God's Will

Zechariah and Elizabeth

Luke 1: 5–25

1:5 In the days of King Herod of Judaea there lived a priest called Zechariah who belonged to the Abijah section of the priesthood, and he had a wife, Elizabeth by name, who was a descendant of Aaron.

1:6 Both were worthy in the sight of God, and scrupulously observed all the commandments and observances of the Lord.

1:7 But they were childless: Elizabeth was barren and they were both getting on in years.

1:8 Now it was the turn of Zechariah's section to serve, and he was exercising his priestly office before God

1:9 when it fell to him by lot, as the ritual custom was, to enter the Lord's sanctuary and burn incense there.

1:10 And at the hour of incense the whole congregation was outside, praying.

1:11 Then there appeared to him the angel of the Lord, standing on the right of the altar of incense.

1:12 The sight disturbed Zechariah and he was overcome with fear.

1:13 But the angel said to him, 'Zechariah, do not be afraid, your prayer has been heard. Your wife Elizabeth is to bear you a son and you must name him John.

1:14 'He will be your joy and delight and many will rejoice at his birth,

1:15 'for he will be great in the sight of the Lord; he must drink no wine, no strong drink. Even from his mother's womb he will be filled with the Holy Spirit,

1:16 'and he will bring back many of the sons of Israel to the Lord their God.

1:17 'With the spirit and power of Elijah, he will go before him to turn the hearts of fathers towards their children and the disobedient back to the wisdom that the virtuous have, preparing for the Lord a people fit for him.'

1:18 Zechariah said to the angel, 'How can I be sure of this? I am an old man and my wife is getting on in years.'

1:19 The angel replied, 'I am Gabriel who stand in God's presence, and I have been sent to speak to you and bring you this good news.

1:20 'Listen! Since you have not believed my words, which will come true at their appointed time, you will be silenced and have no power of speech until this has happened.'

1:21 Meanwhile the people were waiting for Zechariah and were surprised that he stayed in the sanctuary so long.

1:22 When he came out he could not speak to them, and they realised that he had received a vision in the sanctuary. But he could only make signs to them, and remained dumb.

1:23 When his time of service came to an end he returned home.

1:24 Some time later his wife Elizabeth conceived, and for five months she kept to herself.

1:25 'The Lord has done this for me' she said 'now that

it has pleased him to take away the humiliation I suffered among men.'

With God all things are possible. God made the whole world and he loves the whole world. An astonishing aspect of this love, astonishing because it surprises us when we check our own estimations of our own love against its standard, is that **this love allows the world not to love back.** God has given us the power to choose, between himself and ourselves, between good and bad. If we really want to believe in God and want to do what God wants of us, we choose God. We choose what God wants us to do and not what we want to do ourselves. This is much more difficult than we like to think. We often think that we are choosing God, when actually we choosing what we should like God to want.

Zechariah and his wife Elizabeth were both very good people. He served God and the people in the temple. For a long time they had been asking God for a child of their marriage, but they remained childless. Now their part in his plan is revealed to them: God wants Zechariah and Elizabeth to have a child who will turn people's hearts to God, remind people of what they have been told by the prophets and prepare them for the Lord. This child, John, will tell the world about God and ask people to choose God.

How does Zechariah react? He is frightened by the angel. Gabriel who stands 'in the presence of God', is beside him in the temple, much holier and more powerful than the incense and the holy atmosphere. Zechariah is very frightened, but, more than that, he does not really believe what the angel tells him. He is doing his own thinking, not allowing God to be God: 'How shall I know this is true? I am very old and so is my wife.'

The angel is not angry. He tells Zechariah that his message is true and that Elizabeth is going to have the child. Their prayers are answered, even if not in quite the way or at the time they had expected. And to show Zechariah that he means what he says, the angel tells him he will be dumb until the message is proved true.

Elizabeth begins her pregnancy and knows that her prayers have been answered. She thanks God for his kindness. She is getting ready to play her part in God's plan, what he wants for the world and not just for her.

This is the task for each of us: to trust God and to do his will in our lives. If we believe in God, we have to allow God to know best and to accept what happens in our lives, even and particularly when it seems incredible that this is God's will. All this because we believe that God loves us.

12

Mary's Submission to God's Will

The Annunciation

Luke 1: 26–38

1:26 In the sixth month the angel Gabriel was sent by God to a town in Galilee called Nazareth,

1:27 to a virgin betrothed to a man named Joseph, of the House of David; and the virgin's name was Mary.

1:28 He went in and said to her, 'Rejoice, so highly favoured! The Lord is with you.'

1:29 She was deeply disturbed by these words and asked herself what this greeting could mean,

1:30 but the angel said to her, 'Mary, do not be afraid; you have won God's favour.

1:31 'Listen! You are to conceive and bear a son, and you must name him Jesus.

1:32 'He will be great and will be called Son of the Most High. The Lord God will give him the throne of his ancestor David;

1:33 'He will rule over the House of Jacob for ever and his reign will have no end.'

1:34 Mary said to the angel, 'But how can this come about, since I am a virgin?'

1:35 'The Holy Spirit will come upon you' the angel answered 'and the power of the Most High will cover you with its shadow. And so the child will be holy and will be called Son of God.

1:36 'Know this too: your kinswoman Elizabeth has, in her old age, herself conceived a son, and she whom people called barren is now in her sixth month,

1:37 'for nothing is impossible to God.'

1:38 'I am the handmaid of the Lord,' said Mary 'let what you have said be done to me.' And the angel left her.

Mary is told by Gabriel that she is to be the mother of Jesus. Mary, engaged to be married to Joseph whose ancestry traces back to the great king of Israel, King David, is visited by an angel, just as was Zechariah.

How different is Mary's reaction from Zechariah's. Yes, she is afraid too and has to be comforted by the angel. She asks Gabriel to explain how she is to have a child when she is not yet married. But she believes, she does not ask how she is to know that the message is true. **Mary believes this extraordinary message. She accepts: 'Let it be done unto me according to your word.'**

We believe that Mary was holy, that her immaculate conception brought her into the world at her birth **without sin**, and that she lived without sin. Her words to Gabriel are like those of Jesus when he later taught us how to pray and gave us the words of the Our Father: 'Thy will be done'. Her reply to Gabriel expresses this holiness and explains to us all what it means to be holy. **We see that holiness is not about feeling good and doing the good we want to do. Holiness is living God's will, having chosen God and not ourselves.** Mary stands as an inspiration and model for us all: the human without sin or fault, a person in the deepest and truest possible sense, living as God wants each of us to live in this life.

We can remember this scene every time we say the Hail Mary. The prayer begins with Gabriel's greeting. We pray to Mary because we know how close she was to Jesus during his life on earth. She was with him when he died. **In our prayer to Mary, we ask her to pray for us. We know that God will hear her prayers in heaven.**

We ask her to pray for us 'now'. It is now that we need help in choosing God. What happened yesterday is past and who knows what will happen tomorrow? It is now that we face our decision to be like Mary, or not, to say 'Let it be unto me according to your word.'

We also ask Mary to pray for us 'at the hour of our death'. That is the other moment in our lives when we shall need help in choosing God. None of us knows when that moment will come. **We should try to live so that we should be ready to die, and happy to go to God, at any moment.** It is a beautiful prayer and a useful one which the angel began when he spoke to Mary.

13

The Prophetic Prayer of Humility and Faith

The Magnificat

Luke 1: 39–56

1:39   Mary set out at that time and went as quickly as she could to a town in the hill country of Judah.

1:40   She went into Zechariah's house and greeted Elizabeth.

1:41   Now as soon as Elizabeth heard Mary's greeting, the child leapt in her womb and Elizabeth was filled with the Holy Spirit.

1:42   She gave a loud cry and said, 'Of all women you are the most blessed, and blessed is the fruit of your womb.

1:43   'Why should I be honoured with a visit from the mother of my Lord?

1:44   'For the moment your greeting reached my ears, the child in my womb leapt for joy.

1:45 'Yes, blessed is she who believed that the promise made her by the Lord would be fulfilled.'

1:46 And Mary said: 'My soul proclaims the greatness of the Lord

1:47 'and my spirit *exults in God my saviour;*

1:48 'because *he has looked upon his lowly handmaid.* Yes, from this day forward all generations will call me blessed,

1:49 'for the Almighty has done great things for me. *Holy is his name,*

1:50 'and *his mercy reaches from age to age for those who fear him.*

1:51 'He has shown the power of his arm, he has routed the proud of heart.

1:52 '*He has pulled down princes* from their thrones *and exalted the lowly.*

1:53 '*The hungry he has filled with good things,* the rich sent empty away.

1:54 '*He has come to the help of Israel his servant, mindful of his mercy*

1:55 '– according to the *promise he made to our ancestors* – of his mercy to Abraham and to his descendants for ever.'

1:56 Mary stayed with Elizabeth about three months and then went back home.

Mary visits Elizabeth who recognises her as the Mother of God. Mary answers with a prayer, praising God for the grace he has given her and for his mercy to men.

Both women are speaking prophetically – they are proclaiming God's will for the world. Like the prophets of the Old Testament, they speak with conviction and assurance. We cannot of ourselves experience this conviction. It is faith which is the gift of God, always given when asked for, but given in God's own way and in his own good time. This is the work of the Holy Spirit.

We see in Mary's prayer something of what Jesus will mean for the world. Those who are proud of themselves, thinking that it is they, not God, who can do great things, will be lost; those who consider themselves rich will find themselves empty; those who know that before God they are poor, will be lifted up; those who are hungry for what only God can give, will be filled. Jesus will teach these things himself in his Sermon on the Mount (cf. Matthew 5: 1–12 and Luke 6: 20–23)

Mary says that all people will call her blessed. She does not mean herself, Mary, because she is so good, but as a sign which points to God. When we think of Mary, we think of Jesus and his Father in heaven. Her statement is true. Two thousand years later we are indeed calling her blessed. We are praying to her because she helps us understand God the Father in Jesus. And we use in our prayer the words Elizabeth used, 'Blessed art thou among women, and blessed is the fruit of thy womb, Jesus'.

Mary's prayer draws from ancient scripture. In this text from Luke, the passages in italics provide cross references to books in the Old Testament. Rereading the italicised parts, we can compare them with:

1 Samuel 2: 1

Then Hannah said this prayer: 'My heart exults in Yahweh, my horn is exalted in my God, my mouth derides my foes, for I rejoice in your power of saving.'

1 Samuel 1: 11 (from the prayer of Hannah)

(and Hannah) . . . made a vow, saying, 'Yahweh Sabaoth! If you will take notice of the distress of your servant, and bear me in mind and not forget your servant and give her a man-child, I will give him to Yahweh for the whole of his life and no razor shall ever touch his head'.

Psalm 111: 9

Quickly he comes to his people's rescue,
imposing his covenant once and for all;
so holy his name, commanding our dread.

Psalm 103: 17

Yet **Yahweh's love** for those who fear him **lasts from all eternity and for ever, like his goodness to their children's children**.

Job 12: 19

12:19 **He** makes priests walk barefoot, and **overthrows the powers that are established.**

Job 5: 11

If his will is to rescue the downcast, or raise the afflicted to the heights of joy

Psalm 107: 9

satisfying the hungry, he fills the starving with good things.

Psalm 98: 2–3

Yahweh has displayed his power; has revealed his righteousness to the nations, mindful of his love and faithfulness to the House of Israel.

Isaiah 41: 8–9

You, Israel, my servant, Jacob whom I have chosen, descendant of Abraham my friend.

We think of the attention and learning which we would need to extract these references unaided, the familiarity with scripture which could only be born of a great love of it. We may be tempted to think that in some way it was different for Mary. Yet she was quoting from lines written many centuries before her own time. But it is not the literary agility which is so striking. What must be significant for us in reading Mary's prayer is the clear impact she expresses of the God she believes in.

Who is this God whose power she extols and whose grace is particularly close to the poor and the weak? This is a different kind of deity from the projections of our purely human ideas of power. Mary's Magnificat is a song of faith and for us a constant reminder that we must deepen our faith, ever be searching for a deeper openness to God's own mystery. We need that reverence to be receptive to the events which are about to happen. **It is now nearly time for Elizabeth to have her child who will prepare the way for the Son of God, for Jesus whom Mary will bring into the world.**

14

Zechariah's Prophecy

The Birth of John

Luke 1: 57–79

1:57 Meanwhile the time came for Elizabeth to have her child, and she gave birth to a son;

1:58 and when her neighbours and relations heard that the Lord had shown her so great a kindness, they shared her joy.

1:59 Now on the eighth day they came to circumcise the child; they were going to call him Zechariah after his father,

1:60 but his mother spoke up. 'No,' she said 'he is to be called John.'

1:61 They said to her, 'But no one in your family has that name',

1:62 and made signs to his father to find out what he wanted him called.

1:63 The father asked for a writing-tablet and wrote, 'His name is John'. And they were all astonished.

1:64 At that instant his power of speech returned and he spoke and praised God.

1:65 All their neighbours were filled with awe and the

whole affair was talked about throughout the hill country of Judaea.

1:66 All those who heard of it treasured it in their hearts. 'What will this child turn out to be?' they wondered. And indeed the hand of the Lord was with him.

1:67 His father Zechariah was filled with the Holy Spirit and spoke this prophecy:

1:68 'Blessed be the Lord, the God of Israel, for he has visited his people, he has come to their rescue

1:69 'and he has raised up for us a power for salvation in the House of his servant David,

1:70 'even as he proclaimed, by the mouth of his holy prophets from ancient times,

1:71 'that he would save us from our enemies and from the hands of all who hate us.

1:72 'Thus he shows mercy to our ancestors, thus he remembers his holy covenant,

1:73 'the oath he swore to our father Abraham

1:74 'that he would grant us, free from fear, to be delivered from the hands of our enemies,

1:75 'to serve him in holiness and virtue in his presence, all our days.

1:76 'And you, little child, you shall be called Prophet of the Most High, for you will go before the Lord to prepare the way for him.

1:77 'To give his people knowledge of salvation through the forgiveness of their sins;

1:78 'this by the tender mercy of our God who from on high will bring the rising Sun to visit us,

1:79 'to give light to those who live in darkness and the shadow of death, and to guide our feet into the way of peace.'

The message of the angel is true. **Elizabeth has a son** and Zechariah gets back his voice when he confirms that **the child is called John.** The people are afraid and nervous. They ask, 'What will this child be?' Like them, we often do not recognise that God is at work all about us. We too fear the uncertainty in life. We do not in practice trust in God's love for us.

Zechariah's prophecy is in two parts. He says that **God has saved his people so that they may live in holiness, lead the lives he wants for them.** This is again a statement of how much God loves us and cares about us – the most important thing to remember.

Then Zechariah looks into the future and says that **John will teach people about the way God has saved them: his forgiveness of sins.** This is an idea which we come to understand quite slowly as life goes on. We do not usually have a problem with knowing when we have done something wrong. We know when we are choosing not for God, not for others, but for ourselves. We know about conscience. The problem is having confidence in God's forgiveness. A great barrier is our pride which drives our sense of disappointment in ourselves. In crude situations, we may fear punishment. Most usually, we are trying to avoid embarrassment, the loss of esteem and, more specially, self-esteem.

So resilient and subtle are these barriers, it is a wonder that we ever reach out for forgiveness. John's teaching is still contemporary. We still need it because we shirk contact with that forgiveness. Forgiveness opens up a hard path of self-knowledge, a purification which may set us free, but will still cost us much we would rather retain to ourselves.

Finally, Zechariah refers to **a day which will 'give light to those who live in darkness'.** Something immensely important is about to happen which will change the world, bring light to the dark places in the world and in ourselves. **The visits of the angels and the birth of John are all in preparation for this moment. It is the coming of the Son of God.**

15

The Incarnation: A Call to Conversion

The Nativity

Luke 2: 1–20

2:1 Now at this time Caesar Augustus issued a decree for a census of the whole world to be taken.

2:2 This census – the first – took place while Quirinius was governor of Syria,

2:3 and everyone went to his own town to be registered.

2:4 So Joseph set out from the town of Nazareth in Galilee and travelled up to Judaea, to the town of David called Bethlehem, since he was of David's House and line,

2:5 in order to be registered together with Mary, his betrothed, who was with child.

2:6 While they were there the time came for her to have her child,

2:7 and she gave birth to a son, her first born. She wrapped him in swaddling clothes, and laid him in a manger because there was no room for them at the inn.

2:8   In the countryside close by there were shepherds who lived in the fields and took it in turns to watch their flocks during the night.

2:9   The angel of the Lord appeared to them and the glory of the Lord shone round them. They were terrified,

2:10   but the angel said, 'Do not be afraid. Listen, I bring you news of great joy, a joy to be shared by the whole people.

2:11   'Today in the town of David a saviour has been born to you; he is Christ the Lord.

2:12   'And here is a sign for you: you will find a baby wrapped in swaddling clothes and lying in a manger.'

2:13   And suddenly with the angel there was a great throng of the heavenly host, praising God and singing:

2:14   'Glory to God in the highest heaven, and peace to men who enjoy his favour.'

2:15   Now when the angels had gone from them into heaven, the shepherds said to one another, 'Let us go to Bethlehem and see this thing that has happened which the Lord has made known to us.'

2:16   So they hurried away and found Mary and Joseph, and the baby lying in the manger.

2:17   When they saw the child they repeated what they had been told about him,

2:18   and everyone who heard it was astonished at what the shepherds had to say.

2:19   As for Mary, she treasured all these things and pondered them in her heart.

2:20   And the shepherds went back glorifying and praising God for all they had heard and seen; it was exactly as they had been told.

From the first moments of the life of Jesus we are surprised. God reveals himself to the world; he comes into the world to save his people. And which of us would have guessed that he would do it in this way? Imagine the might and power of the Roman empire. The emperor, Caesar Augustus, one of the greatest of the Roman emperors, decides to count all the people in his empire and makes them all go to the towns and cities where they belong. And **God comes into the world, a helpless child for whom there is no room.** He is born where the animals are being kept. We may be so used to the Nativity story that we have lost hold of the astonishing paradox of what is taking place. From the very beginning, is not Jesus telling us that we have to put aside our own ideas of God?

So different from the reflexes of our own imagination, were we able to imagine how God might appear to the world, his incarnation is in the form of an infant. He comes down to us, in search of us, and is present among us as a child. By choosing a human birth he utterly embraces our human situation, in all things but sin. **We are to feel at ease with this God.**

The news is first given to shepherds on the hill. Only in the way the message is given them, do we see hints of how great and beautiful is the event: an angel and a great crowd of the heavenly host, singing God's praise. And the shepherds understood. Can we begin to imagine their faces in this scene?

It is important in learning about the life of Jesus to remind ourselves that we are learning about things which really did happen, even if they were a very long time ago. We can put ourselves into those events and imagine how we ourselves would have thought and behaved if we had been there. This helps us to learn more about what happened and to see that these events have an actual meaning for our own lives.

In this way, we should all, like the shepherds, say, 'Let us go over to Bethlehem and see this thing that has happened.' Let us make this journey into the life of Jesus. **We have to go over from where we are now. We have to go over to where he is, and make a real effort to see what Jesus**

74

is like and what it is he is saying to us, to find him, not as a concept, but as a reality.

When we do this, we remember the example of Mary. She is always there too. Like her, let us keep all these things, pondering them in our hearts.

16

Prophetic Greetings

The Magi and Simeon

Matthew 2: 1–12

2:1 After Jesus had been born at Bethlehem in Judaea during the reign of King Herod, some wise men came to Jerusalem from the east.

2:2 'Where is the infant king of the Jews?' they asked. 'We saw his star as it rose and have come to do him homage.'

2:3 When King Herod heard this he was perturbed, and so was the whole of Jerusalem.

2:4 He called together all the chief priests and the scribes of the people, and enquired of them where the Christ was to be born.

2:5 'At Bethlehem in Judaea,' they told him 'for this is what the prophet wrote:

2:6 "And you, Bethlehem, in the land of Judah, you are by no means least among the leaders of Judah, for out of you will come a leader who will shepherd my people Israel".'

2:7 Then Herod summoned the wise men to see him privately. He asked them the exact date on which the star had appeared,

2:8   and sent them on to Bethlehem. 'Go and find out all about the child,' he said 'and when you have found him, let me know, so that I too may go and do him homage.'

2:9   Having listened to what the king had to say, they set out. And there in front of them was the star they had seen rising; it went forward, and halted over the place where the child was.

2:10   The sight of the star filled them with delight,

2:11   and going into the house they saw the child with his mother Mary, and falling to their knees they did him homage. Then, opening their treasures, they offered him gifts of gold and frankincense and myrrh.

2:12   But they were warned in a dream not to go back to Herod, and returned to their own country by a different way.

Luke 2: 21–35

2:21   When the eighth day came and the child was to be circumcised, they gave him the name Jesus, the name the angel had given him before his conception.

2:22   And when the day came for them to be purified as laid down by the Law of Moses, they took him up to Jerusalem to present him to the Lord –

2:23   observing what stands written in the Law of the Lord: Every first-born male must be consecrated to the Lord –

2:24   and also to offer in sacrifice, in accordance with what is said in the Law of the Lord, a pair of turtledoves or two young pigeons.

2:25   Now in Jerusalem there was a man named Simeon. He was an upright and devout man; he looked forward to Israel's comforting and the Holy Spirit rested on him.

2:26   It had been revealed to him by the Holy Spirit that he would not see death until he had set eyes on the Christ of the Lord.

2:27 Prompted by the Spirit he came to the Temple; and when the parents brought in the child Jesus to do for him what the Law required,

2:28 he took him into his arms and blessed God; and he said:

2:29 'Now, Master, you can let your servant go in peace, just as you promised;

2:30 'because my eyes have seen the salvation

2:31 'which you have prepared for all the nations to see,

2:32 'a light to enlighten the pagans and the glory of your people Israel.'

2:33 As the child's father and mother stood there wondering at the things that were being said about him,

2:34 Simeon blessed them and said to Mary his mother, 'You see this child: he is destined for the fall and for the rising of many in Israel, destined to be a sign that is rejected –

2:35 and a sword will pierce your own soul too – so that the secret thoughts of many may be laid bare.'

These two passages tell us how **Jesus was recognised as the Christ in the first days of his life by the great of the earth, the three wise men, and by Simeon, the priest in the temple.**

Traditionally the three wise men are often remembered as kings called Melchior, Balthazar and Caspar. We do not know where they came from, but 'the east' calls to mind ancient civilisations and learning. We celebrate the coming of the wise men as a feast day, the Epiphany – the revealing of the infant Christ to the gentiles, the non-Jewish peoples of the world. **The three wise men represent the gentile world; they represent us.**

The prophecy of which the priests and scribes remind Herod comes from the prophet Micah who had lived in the Holy Land seven hundred years before (Micah 5:1).

**The wise men's presents are symbolic. Gold is pure
and precious, the sign of a king; frankincense is from
the gum of a tree and is burnt in holy places, a sign
of holiness; myrrh is an aromatic resin, used to
embalm the dead, a sign here of how Jesus is to die.**

The priest Simeon, rather like Zechariah, had been told in a
dream that he would not die before he had seen the Christ,
promised in scripture. We may imagine this holy old man,
patiently waiting to be released from the burden of old age
by God's promise, and his feelings on seeing Jesus. His gentle prayer recognises God's purpose that Jesus is come to save
the world. Then **Simeon** speaks prophetically to Mary. He
**tells her the coming of Jesus will cause great discord
in Israel as not all will believe in him.** Mary herself will
suffer as Jesus is rejected by his own people.

These two encounters complete the supernatural story of
Jesus' birth. They balance, with a note of vast splendour, the
intimate circumstances of the stable where he was born. The
child in the manger is marked with a star and recognised by
grave men from a far country and by a holy man in the temple of God. Man the worker, the farmer, the father of a family, Man the thinker and ruler, and Man the servant of God,
each encounters the Incarnate God; we encounter in the
image of ourselves the divine nature; the divine nature
comes in search of us humbly lest we be afraid.

17

Jesus' Vocation

Jesus in the Temple

Luke 2: 41–52

2:41 Every year his parents used to go to Jerusalem for the feast of the Passover.

2:42 When he was twelve years old, they went up for the feast as usual.

2:43 When they were on their way home after the feast, the boy Jesus stayed behind in Jerusalem without his parents knowing it.

2:44 They assumed he was with the caravan, and it was only after a day's journey that they went to look for him among their relations and acquaintances.

2:45 When they failed to find him they went back to Jerusalem looking for him everywhere.

2:46 Three days later, they found him in the Temple, sitting among the doctors, listening to them, and asking them questions;

2:47 and all those who heard him were astounded at his intelligence and his replies.

2:48 They were overcome when they saw him, and his mother said to him, 'My child, why have you done this to us? See how worried your father and I have been, looking for you.'

2:49 'Why were you looking for me?' he replied 'Did you not know that I must be busy with my Father's affairs?'

2:50 But they did not understand what he meant.

2:51 He then went down with them and came to Nazareth and lived under their authority. His mother stored up all these things in her heart.

2:52 And Jesus increased in wisdom, in stature, and in favour with God and men.

Jesus has been seen by the simple shepherds at his birth, he has been visited by the three kings and has been recognised by Simeon in the temple. Now **Jesus, no longer a tiny baby, but a boy, presents himself to the people in the temple.** He discusses with the learned men and they too are amazed, but we are not told that they recognise him as their Lord, the Son of God.

Why did Jesus go back to the temple? In his answer to his mother, 'I must be busy with my Father's affairs', we can see the longing which even a child has for what is good and holy. **We also see the beginnings of his own realisation that he has a mission in life, a task which only he can fulfil**, and that he must take to it. Young people are like this. Their difficulty is defining what is the right thing to do next in order to answer this sense of being called to something greater, something over there. We cannot tell how Jesus understood his future. If we believe in his true humanity, that he was true Man and true God, then we see him here reaching out for something which he senses lies ahead, which conforms to his Father's will.

Why did Jesus upset his parents by going back without telling them where he was going? Like his parents, this is how we too see his behaviour. They were upset for a

81

while because they did not understand. Jesus' answer to his mother tells us that he did not mean to upset her. **He says that he must be first in his Father's house, that what he owes his Father comes before what he might owe anybody else. This is true also of us. Saying 'Yes' to God must come before all things.**

Jesus returns home with Mary and Joseph and shows us in doing so that **his 'Yes' to his Father also meant living obediently with his parents.**

Mary and Joseph do not understand what Jesus tells them, just as we often do not understand what God is saying to us in our families and lives. But they do not dismiss what they cannot understand. Mary, just as she considered Gabriel's message in her mind, 'kept all these things in her heart'. Such was Mary's faith. She accepts what is difficult, even if she cannot at the time understand it. All parents suffer in this way as their children grow up. Mary's example helps us to trust and accept God's will that each of us is first his – 'for he loved us first' (1 John 4:10) and only each other's because we are his.

18

John's Teaching and the Baptism of the Lamb of God

John meets Jesus

Matthew 3: 1–17

3:1   In due course John the Baptist appeared; he preached in the wilderness of Judaea and this was his message:

3:2   'Repent, for the kingdom of heaven is close at hand.'

3:3   This was the man the prophet Isaiah spoke of when he said: 'A voice cries in the wilderness. Prepare a way for the Lord, make his paths straight.'

3:4   This man John wore a garment made of camel-hair with a leather belt round his waist, and his food was locusts and wild honey.

3:5   Then Jerusalem and all Judaea and the whole Jordan district made their way to him,

3:6   and as they were baptised by him in the river Jordan they confessed their sins.

3:7   But when he saw a number of Pharisees and Sadducees coming for baptism he said to them,

3:8   'Brood of vipers, who warned you to fly from the retribution that is coming? But if you are repentant, produce the appropriate fruit,

3:9 'and do not presume to tell yourselves, "We have Abraham for our father", because, I tell you, God can raise children for Abraham from these stones.

3:10 'Even now the axe is laid to the roots of the trees, so that any tree which fails to produce good fruit will be cut down and thrown on the fire.

3:11 'I baptise you in water for repentance, but the one who follows me is more powerful than I am, and I am not fit to carry his sandals; he will baptise you with the Holy Spirit and fire.

3:12 'His winnowing-fan is in his hand; he will clear his threshing-floor and gather his wheat into the barn; but the chaff he will burn in a fire that will never go out.'

3:13 Then Jesus appeared: he came from Galilee to the Jordan to be baptised by John.

3:14 John tried to dissuade him. 'It is I who need baptism from you' he said 'and yet you come to me!'

3:15 But Jesus replied, 'Leave it like this for the time being; it is fitting that we should, in this way, do all that righteousness demands'. At this, John gave in to him.

3:16 As soon as Jesus was baptised he came up from the water, and suddenly the heavens opened and he saw the Spirit of God descending like a dove and coming down on him.

3:17 And a voice spoke from heaven, 'This is my Son, the Beloved; my favour rests on him'.

John, as the angel promised to his father Zechariah, is grown up to be a man of God, preaching to the people, telling them that they must prepare for the coming of one greater than himself. John tells them to repent – to consider the sins and wrong things they have done – and to be truly sorry for them. **He teaches that God wants to forgive man his sins, but we can only enter into this forgiveness by recognising our sins and being sorry for them. John baptises his followers with water as a sign that their sins are washed away by God's forgiveness.**

John is causing quite a stir in Judaea and is questioned by the Pharisees and Sadducees who do not believe in him, because they are sure that they are right and do not need his message. **John reminds them that man cannot be confident of his own righteousness before God. He uses the images of the fruit tree, of the harvest, the threshing floor and the winnowing fork to tell them that it is God who will judge our worth, not us.**

John is asked if he is the Christ expected by the prophets of the Old Testament. He is adamant that he is not, and speaks of one coming after him beside whom he will be as nothing. John in his life of self-denial and simplicity is a wonderful example of humility: his eye and his heart are set on the greatness of God and not on himself. He recognises that all that is important is God and that therefore he himself is unimportant. This is only comprehensible to us if we reflect how close John must have been to God. We go so far with our praise of God's greatness, but when it begins to cut into our own understanding of ourselves, it often tapers off: the stress is great. By keeping his eye on God and not on himself, John perceived something of God's nature. his deductions about himself then became natural.

Jesus comes to be baptised, not because he needs forgiveness, but because he knows John is doing God's work. John's recognition of Jesus, the vision of the Holy Spirit and the voice of God from the heavens announce Jesus to the people. Jesus' ministry now begins. To the end of his time on earth he is teaching and healing. He is preparing his followers for his death and resurrection. John's mission and his encounter with Jesus allow us to listen directly to God as Jesus comes into our lives.

In John's Gospel (John 1:29), John the Baptist exclaims when he sees Jesus, 'Look, there is the Lamb of God that takes away the sin of the world.' Only the authority of ancient scripture can help us with this astonishing statement. What unfathomable thoughts must have occurred to a bystander who heard these words and looked up and into the face of Jesus? At the very outset of Jesus' ministry, John links the ancient religious beliefs of his people with Jesus' ultimate fate, identifying in this single sentence the heart of God the Father's will to secure the salvation of mankind in the sacrificial mystery of his Son. We use this sentence of John's in our prayer at Mass just before receiving Holy Communion.

19

Vocation: Conversion to a New Life in Christ

Jesus calls his Disciples

Mark 1: 16–20

1:16 As he was walking along by the Sea of Galilee he saw Simon and his brother Andrew casting a net in the lake – for they were fishermen.

1:17 And Jesus said to them, 'Follow me and I will make you into fishers of men.'

1:18 And at once they left their nets and followed him.

1:19 Going on a little further, he saw James son of Zebedee and his brother John; they too were in their boat, mending their nets. He called them at once

1:20 and, leaving their father Zebedee in the boat with the men he employed, they went after him.

Luke 5: 1–11

5:1 Now he was standing one day by the Lake of Gennesaret, with the crowd pressing round him listening to the word of God,

5:2   when he caught sight of two boats close to the bank. The fishermen had gone out of them and were washing their nets.

5:3   He got into one of the boats – it was Simon's – and asked him to put out a little from the shore. Then he sat down and taught the crowds from the boat.

5:4   When he had finished speaking he said to Simon, 'Put out into deep water and pay out your nets for a catch'.

5:5   'Master,' Simon replied 'we worked hard all night long and caught nothing, but if you say so, I will pay out the nets.'

5:6   And when they had done this they netted such a huge number of fish that their nets began to tear,

5:7   so they signalled to their companions in the other boat to come and help them; when these came, they filled the two boats to sinking point.

5:8   When Simon Peter saw this he fell at the knees of Jesus saying, 'Leave me, Lord; I am a sinful man'.

5:9   For he and all his companions were completely overcome by the catch they had made;

5:10   so also were James and John, sons of Zebedee, who were Simon's partners. But Jesus said to Simon, 'Do not be afraid; from now on it is men you will catch'.

5:11   Then, bringing their boats back to land, they left everything and followed him.

Jesus has begun to teach the people, as John the Baptist had been teaching them before him. By the lakeside, **he now calls to him the first of those who will follow him through to the end of his life**, and who later will be reunited with their risen Lord in a very similar scene by the shore of the lake when he will give them bread and fish to eat, asking them to feed his lambs (John 21: 1–19).

A disciple is one who learns from a teacher. Jesus calls ordinary working men, fishermen to be his disciples. **Jesus' call is to all of us and each of us.** We may appear ordinary to each other, but each of us is special to him. The disciples will help Jesus with his work and continue it after his death and resurrection. They become fishers of men, bringing the souls of men to the Father who is in Heaven.

In Jesus' call to the disciples, in his teaching and their work together, in their friendship, we see the beginning of the Church. We are members of the same Church as the disciples; Jesus offers us the same friendship.

Jesus reveals himself to the disciples in the marvellous catch of fish. How does Simon Peter react to this? He sees that the fish are a sign. He recognises the goodness of Jesus. This makes him reflect on himself and realise how far short he is himself of that goodness, how sinful he is. We often hear in the Gospels of people saying how sinful they are; the saints often say the same. This is not so much a statement that they know that they are very wicked and evil people by comparison with anybody else. Such comparisons are not useful. Instead, they see their own failings because they are near to Jesus – the comparison is of the human with the absolute goodness of the incarnate Word. Simon Peter with Jesus beside him was aware of who Jesus was, and what sort of person he was himself. Jesus' goodness is the way to understand ourselves.

What does Jesus say next to Simon Peter? He tells him not to be afraid. We remember the angel saying the same to Zechariah, to Mary and to the shepherds. This power and goodness which are God's are full of love. Jesus' love is not turned away by sinfulness. His response to the sinner is not reproach, but love. Jesus knows what self-knowledge costs us, how destabilising and depressing it can be. He sees its sense of isolation, its panic. In these moments, we know we need help, even saving. He offers his love to save us. He tells us not to be afraid to be loved by him, not to be afraid to respond to that vocation which he addresses individually to each of us, that we live in his love.

20

Christ's Gift of Himself

The Wedding at Cana

John 2: 1–11

2:1 Three days later there was a wedding at Cana in Galilee. The mother of Jesus was there,

2:2 and Jesus and his disciples had also been invited.

2:3 When they ran out of wine, since the wine provided for the wedding was all finished, the mother of Jesus said to him, 'They have no wine.'

2:4 Jesus said 'Woman, why turn to me? My hour has not come yet.'

2:5 His mother said to the servants, 'Do whatever he tells you.'

2:6 There were six stone water jars standing there, meant for the ablutions that are customary among the Jews: each could hold twenty or thirty gallons.

2:7 Jesus said to the servants, 'Fill the jars with water', and they filled them to the brim.

2:8 'Draw some out now' he told them 'and take it to the steward.'

2:9 They did this; the steward tasted the water, and it had turned into wine. Having no idea where it came from – only the servants who had drawn the water knew – the steward called the bridegroom

2:10 and said, 'People generally serve the best wine first, and keep the cheaper sort till the guests have had plenty to drink; but you have kept the best wine till now.'

2:11 This was the first of the signs given by Jesus: it was given at Cana in Galilee. He let his glory be seen, and his disciples believed in him.

Jesus and his mother are at a wedding feast and, at such a proud moment for the bride and groom, the wine runs out. This would be bad enough for any of us. In the culture of the Near East, however, enormous emphasis is laid on the virtues of generosity and hospitality. A host who does not provide for his guests gives truly shocking offence. Mary knows her son and knows that he can save the day. **It appears that he had no thought to reveal himself and he tells his mother so.** We notice that he does not refuse to help and when his mother gives instructions to the servants, **he is obedient.** He helps when he is asked to. **When the servants draw the water from the huge jars, and take it to the steward, it is wonderful wine.**

The steward does not know what Jesus has done, but his comment to the bridegroom tells us something important about Jesus: **in life the best is yet to come.** We usually want the best now. If, however, we put up with difficulties now, Jesus will show us what he is keeping for us until the last. Secondly, the **bridegroom has the benefit of Jesus' wonderful work without realising it. God is always with us in life.** We should learn to recognise that all the good things we enjoy, are there because God wants us to have them.

John tells us that this was the first of Jesus' signs and the disciples believed in him. Jesus' miracles are signs that he is God and that his love for us wants to seek us out, to help us believe in him. He knows how weak our faith is. He knows it takes a miracle to get people to believe.

There are two difficult themes here. We believe that faith, our belief that Jesus Christ is the Son of God, is itself a gift of God. It is a gift God wants us to have, but we cannot have it without his grace. At the same time, as a consequence of our free will, our faith will not deepen and grow unless we actively respond to the gift, do our bit to accept it and let it do its work in our personalities and the way we live.

Secondly, the gift of faith is the gift of Jesus: Jesus' gift of himself, his presence in our lives. This is almost too much to take in at first. We have to work our way through the levels of meaning which are contained in the words and signs which Jesus uses. His signs point to that reality which he is so anxious his disciples should perceive: the eternal life of the soul, a spiritual dimension which informs every aspect of daily existence, God's dimension because, as Jesus teaches us, the Father is spirit.

This miracle foreshadows his last gift to the disciples and to us when he took the wine at the Last Supper, the day before he died, and gave it to them saying it was his blood. The same miracle occurs at Mass when the priest takes the wine into the chalice and it becomes Jesus' blood. This miracle of the Mass helps us to believe and come closer to Jesus, just as the miracle at Cana helped the disciples.

The miracle, just as for the bridegroom, takes place independently of our conscious awareness. The miracle of the Mass does sanctify our lives whether we say to ourselves that we can understand this, or not. Mary's faith was sure, whether or not she was aware of what was about to happen. When we read these accounts of Jesus' miracles, we can use them in our own reflections on our own experience to open ourselves to the gift of a deeper faith and to Jesus' own gift of himself to us.

21

Born of the Spirit in Baptism

Jesus and the Children

Matthew 19: 13–15

19:13 People brought little children to him, for him to lay his hands on them and say a prayer. The disciples turned them away,

19:14 but Jesus said, 'Let the little children alone, and do not stop them coming to me; for it is to such as these that the kingdom of heaven belongs.'

19:15 Then he laid his hands on them and went on his way.

Mark 10: 13–16

10:13 People were bringing little children to him, for him to touch them. The disciples turned them away,

10:14 but when Jesus saw this he was indignant and said to them, 'Let the little children come to me; do not stop them; for it is to such as these that the kingdom of God belongs.

10:15 'I tell you solemnly, anyone who does not welcome the kingdom of God like a little child will never enter it.'

10:16 Then he put his arms round them, laid his hands on them and gave them his blessing.

Luke 18: 15–17

18:15 People even brought little children to him, for him to touch them; but when the disciples saw this they turned them away.

18:16 But Jesus called the children to him and said, 'Let the little children come to me, and do not stop them; for it is to such as these that the kingdom of God belongs.

18:17 'I tell you solemnly, anyone who does not welcome the kingdom of God like a little child will never enter it.'

Wherever Jesus goes, people come to listen to his teaching. He is healing the sick, those who are ill and those who are unhappy. People want him to touch them and to pray for them. **Now they even bring their children so that he may touch them. The disciples are cross about this.** Probably the children are making a noise and making it difficult for the grown-ups to hear. Do they think the people are being superstitious, wanting to draw some magic power from the miracle worker? But Jesus says, **'Let the little children come to me, and do not stop them.'** Jesus likes children; he understands them and wants to help them too.

He then steps behind whatever the disciples' objections may have been. He says something which may have surprised them. He says that the kingdom of God belongs to people just like these children.

Do we really have in our noisy and tiring children models of holiness? What are we to learn from their naturalness and uncomplicated openness to love? Do we sense something of whatever we have understood of the relationship of Adam and Eve with God in their early days in Eden – that powerful image of humanity walking in the friendship of

God? Do the quick generosity of a child and its sense of mystery and awe make us aware of parts of us which we may feel we have lost? This kingdom of God is not just the hereafter, conditions which may or may not apply at an unforeseeable time beyond time. Perhaps it can be now. Perhaps the life of a saint and aspects of the nature of a child are moments of access to the action of the kingdom of God today. Jesus' brief comment to the disciples resonates in our experience and illuminates our relationships with each other.

Each of the three synoptic Gospels gives us an account of this scene. Did the Galileans those centuries ago also revere that straight-laced dictum that children should be 'seen and not heard'? While reflecting on the muddle and wrong turnings of our own efforts to be good parents, it is worth noticing that in Matthew and Mark this scene immediately follows, and in Luke (16:18) follows very shortly after, Jesus' plain words about the sanctity of marriage and its indissolubility.

We need not in these scenes, through fear of sentimentality, turn our backs on the first meanings which may occur to us. It is not just an ideal, but an imperative that we respect children as persons created in God's image. Jesus is also pointing to our need, like children, to be aware of our parents and the fourth commandment.

Most importantly, his language points also to the need for each of us, just as a child seeks out its parents, always to seek out our Father who is in heaven. Sacramentally our birth in the spirit dates from baptism. Our growth in the spirit, as we know from our own experience and from the lives of the saints, follows no programme of earthly ageing. Here we are already in touch with eternity, in the consequences of our actions and in the range of our aspirations. Jesus in this scene with the children is also speaking of this new and spiritual life to which we are heirs through faith and baptism (cf. 1 Peter 1:3, 23 and Paul's letter to Titus, 3:5) 'In truth I tell you no one can enter the kingdom of God without being born through water and the Spirit; what is born of human nature is human; what is born of the Spirit is spirit' (John 3:5). In this rebirth we become, need to become, as children: aware of our smallness in the face of the vastness of God's own reality and self, but nonetheless, like all children loved by their parents, we are to be confident.

The adult parental mind may see the poignancy in Matthew's note that Jesus 'went away'. And so it may often feel for us as self-centred children in the life of the spirit. Then we learn that he never does; his absolute and immediate presence is the ultimate security of the Christian which derives from the promises of Christ, given and believed on the dimension of faith.

22

Weakness an Author of Evil

The Death of John the Baptist

Mark 6: 17–29

6:17 Now it was this same Herod who had sent to have
John arrested, and had him chained up in prison
because of Herodias, his brother Philip's wife whom
he had married.

6:18 For John had told Herod, 'It is against the law for you
to have your brother's wife.'

6:19 As for Herodias, she was furious with him and wanted to kill him; but she was not able to,

6:20 because Herod was afraid of John, knowing him to be
a good and holy man, and gave him his protection.
When he had heard him speak he was greatly per-
plexed, and yet he liked to listen to him.

6:21 An opportunity came on Herod's birthday when he
gave a banquet for the nobles of his court, for his
army officers and for the leading figures in Galilee.

6:22 When the daughter of this same Herodias came in
and danced, she delighted Herod and his guests; so the
king said to the girl, 'Ask me anything you like and I
will give it you.'

6:23 And he swore her an oath, 'I will give you anything you ask, even half my kingdom.'

6:24 She went out and said to her mother, 'What shall I ask for?' She replied, 'The head of John the Baptist.'

6:25 The girl hurried straight back to the king and made her request, 'I want you to give me John the Baptist's head, here and now, on a dish.'

6:26 The king was deeply distressed but, thinking of the oaths he had sworn and of his guests, he was reluctant to break his word to her.

6:27 So the king at once sent one of the bodyguard with orders to bring John's head.

6:28 The man went off and beheaded him in prison; then he brought the head on a dish and gave it to the girl, and the girl gave it to her mother.

6:29 When John's disciples heard about this, they came and took his body and laid it in a tomb.

John, who came into the world to prepare us for the coming of Christ, now foreshadows the death of Jesus with his own death at the hands of Herod and Herodias. The appalling violence of this drama and the familiarity of the story can dull us to its resonance in the world of today and indeed in our own lives. The story teaches us so much about sin.

Consider Herod. Wicked – yes: he took his brother's wife, but isn't the root of his wickedness just familiar weakness? Herodias was probably a very remarkable and strong personality and, if her daughter, Salome, was anyone to judge by, she was also extremely attractive. Herod, under her influence, felt he could not hold to what he knew was right. He abdicates, not his throne – doubtless Herod was a shrewd and forceful ruler – but his will-power. And probably he thinks this does not matter much. He likely comforts himself that he is quite able to distinguish between matters of state which 'really matter' to him, and his 'purely private' affair in taking his brother's wife. And so as a person he is living in moral disorder and he knows this, not least on account of his conversations with John in the prison. And John's message is of repentance which is just what Herod is unable to bring himself to accept. Repentance would mean decisions about Herodias, a crisis for Herod's weakness which he cannot confront. We are all sinful. The question is whether we turn to the Father in sorrow, seeking help, or duck that moment of truth about ourselves.

Secondly, in this murder of John, there is a vicious unaccountability. Everyone can point to everyone else. Herod makes an extravagant offer not expecting it to be taken up in this way; Salome's request is prompted by her mother; the soldier who kills John does so obeying orders. It does us no harm to reflect on the incalculable consequences of even 'small sins' and how they ricochet and precipitate other, perhaps more serious, more terrible wrongs. This knowledge of our actual natures, how we actually stand before God, is the vital challenge, the theme of that beautiful precept from Psalm 110 and the Book of Proverbs: 'Fear of the Lord is the beginning of Wisdom.' For wisdom here is a manifestation, an expression, like the Word, of the mind of the Father. So in our accepting admission of what we are really like, we put ourselves directly in touch with our God. And God forgives our sins. The sacrifice of Christ makes that true. The Mass, which we begin with our confession of our sins, is the eternal sacrifice of Jesus. Our part is to be open to the faith which enables us to accept this.

23

Configuring Tradition to the Paschal Mystery

The Feeding of the Five Thousand

John 6: 1–15

6:1 Some time after this, Jesus went off to the other side of the Sea of Galilee – or of Tiberias –

6:2 and a large crowd followed him, impressed by the signs he gave by curing the sick.

6:3 Jesus climbed the hillside, and sat down there with his disciples.

6:4 It was shortly before the Jewish feast of Passover.

6:5 Looking up, Jesus saw the crowds approaching and said to Philip, 'Where can we buy some bread for these people to eat?'

6:6 He only said this to test Philip; he himself knew exactly what he was going to do.

6:7 Philip answered, 'Two hundred denarii would only buy enough to give them a small piece each'.

6:8 One of his disciples, Andrew, Simon Peter's brother, said,

6:9 'There is a small boy here with five barley loaves and two fish; but what is that between so many?'

6:10 Jesus said to them, 'Make the people sit down'. There was plenty of grass there, and as many as five thousand men sat down.

6:11 Then Jesus took the loaves, gave thanks, and gave them out to all who were sitting ready; he then did the same with the fish, giving out as much as was wanted.

6:12 When they had eaten enough he said to the disciples, 'Pick up the pieces left over, so that nothing gets wasted'.

6:13 So they picked them up, and filled twelve hampers with scraps left over from the meal of five barley loaves.

6:14 The people, seeing this sign that he had given, said, 'This really is the prophet who is to come into the world'.

6:15 Jesus, who could see they were about to come and take him by force and make him king, escaped back to the hills by himself.

At the first Passover in Exodus, God warned Moses to make his people prepare a special sacrificial supper of roast lamb and to mark the doors of their houses with some of the lamb's blood. When the angel of Death passed over the land, he left safe those in the houses with the doors marked, and they were able to escape across the Red Sea into the desert of Sinai and toward the Promised Land. In the desert of their freedom, the people were hungry and God sent them a miraculous food which they found lying on the desert floor and which they called Manna.

When Jesus was with the five thousand near the time of the feast, this early history from the Old Testament would have been remembered. **Jesus' miracle is thus not only a straightforward act of love and care for those in need, but it gives a radical and new meaning to what had happened in the past.** This radical renewal of tradition, this renewal of the people's understanding not only of themselves, but of God and his law, is thematic to Jesus's ministry.

The God of Moses is now among us. He himself is feeding us. His presence among us, the historical event of the incarnation, gives new and dramatic depth to the old understanding of the flight from Egypt as marking the watershed of a people's history, their passing from serfdom to a new life of freedom. **He makes an invitation to an interior conversion in each individual who hears his word.**

The miracle also looks forward to the Last Supper when Jesus gives the disciples bread and wine which he had turned into his own body and blood, a miracle which we have before us every time we go to Mass. At Mass the priest gives us the new Manna of our own rescue from the desert, the desert of sin and our living without God. **He gives us the meal which Jesus gave to this crowd of listeners.**

The five thousand, when they saw what Jesus had done, did not at once recognise him as the Son of God. **Instead they** thought he was a prophet and **wanted to make him king.** How easy it is for us to see how mistaken they were. If Jesus had wanted to be a king, that is how he would have come into the world. At the same time, our own understanding is obscure: we concentrate on what we want to hear. Notice that **Jesus does not argue with the crowd, but departs to the hills 'by himself'** – a phrase which recurs time and again in the Gospels when we see Jesus retiring to pray.

So Jesus does not argue with us when we are mistaken. The only way we can be sure of coming closer to him and to understanding him better, is to stay with him and to allow him to stay with us, following and listening to what it is he is actually saying to us. We do this, as Jesus did with his Father, by going alone into the hills of our souls and listening for him, without any actual expectation of being able to hear and register his speaking to us. We recognise God's action in our lives in retrospect and in our own slow conformation to his will. No doubt individuals among that huge crowd pondered on what had happened, and reflected that in this event indeed God had been among them. This, to the eye of faith, is the constant reality of life.

The recurrent symbolism of fish in these scenes in the Gospel complements the symbol of bread. The Greek word used for fish in this passage (OPSARION) is not the common one. The commoner word (ICHTHUS) was used by the early Christians as an acronym for their faith: Jesus Christ Son of God Saviour (in Greek: IESOUS CHRISTOS THEOU UIOS SOTER). Thus in this miracle prefiguring the Mass, Jesus gives the people bread and himself and his mission. The common food of the lake men is again transfigured when he commissions the disciples after the Resurrection (John 21: 1–19).

24

Love Which Knows and Cares

The Lost Sheep

Matthew 18: 12–14

18:12 'Tell me. Suppose a man has a hundred sheep and one of them strays; will he not leave the ninety-nine on the hillside and go in search of the stray?

18:13 'I tell you solemnly, if he finds it, it gives him more joy than do the ninety-nine that did not stray at all.

18:14 'Similarly, it is never the will of your Father in heaven that one of these little ones should be lost.'

Luke 15: 4–7

15:4 'What man among you with a hundred sheep, losing one, would not leave the ninety-nine in the wilderness and go after the missing one till he found it?

15:5 'And when he found it, would he not joyfully take it on his shoulders

15:6 'and then, when he got home, call together his friends and neighbours? "Rejoice with me," he would say "I have found my sheep that was lost."

15:7 'In the same way, I tell you, there will be more rejoicing in heaven over one repentant sinner than over ninety-nine virtuous men who have no need of repentance.'

Here Jesus is talking about us, telling us that each and every one of us, no matter how small, is of importance to him and to God – our angels behold the face of the Father in heaven. **Jesus gives us a picture of the love he has for us in the image of the shepherd.**

The shepherd is no longer a familiar figure to most of us. In the Holy Land at the time of Jesus, there were no fenced fields for livestock, just open country where the shepherd would lead the sheep out to find grazing, before gathering them up together for the night. He carried a crook to separate and count the sheep, and to catch one up if he wanted to have a close look at it. Sheep can be wayward and they are not easy to catch. They have, in fact, a marked intelligence for their own purposes. But these are often not the same as their shepherd's.

To most of us a flock of sheep is a mass of animals, like a large crowd of people seen from a high window, each individual looking much like another. **To the shepherd, however, each one is known and has its own value.** If he loses one, he searches for it until he finds it. The shepherds in our own hill country in the days before mechanisation would be responsible for a 'cut' of a hundred and fifty sheep. The shepherd would know each sheep and its relations back for several generations.

Jesus is our shepherd and we are his sheep. His love is special for each of us, not just for us in general. And when Jesus tells us to love one another, he means we should love in this way also. **We should love not just in principle, but in particular.**

This love is generous and forgiving. John the Baptist called people to repent of their sins and turn back to God. Jesus says that when the shepherd finds his lost sheep, he is glad. We choose God again and say we are sorry for our turning away; he is glad and tells us that there is 'joy in heaven'. Like the shepherd, it is not his Father's will 'that one of these little ones should perish'.

25

Love Which Restlessly Seeks the Beloved

The Lost Coin

Luke 15: 8–10

15:8 'Or again, what woman with ten drachmas would not, if she lost one, light a lamp and sweep out the house and search thoroughly till she found it?

15:9 'And then, when she had found it, call together her friends and neighbours? "Rejoice with me," she would say "I have found the drachma I lost."

15:10 'In the same way, I tell you, there is rejoicing among the angels of God over one repentant sinner.'

As another way of understanding his love and desire to forgive, Jesus offers us the image of a woman looking for a lost coin, an image familiar to all of us. We can easily see the sweeping and dusting of the house, the tidying up and switching on and off of lights. The search is relentless. Jesus never tires to be near to us when we stray, to be there ready for our turning to him.

Ancient coins were made of precious metals, silver and gold.

If silver is not used and kept clean by rubbing, it tarnishes and becomes black. The oxidisation is on the surface; inside the coin is still silver and bright. The coin lost by the woman may have been missing for some time and when she finds it, it may be black and grimy, covered in dust. This does not diminish its value to her or lessen her gladness in finding it again. It can soon be cleaned up.

That voice which questions us, 'Is this right?' we call our conscience. **The more we try to do what is right**, and to put out of our minds thoughts which are not right, **the clearer our conscience becomes in speaking to us.** It is almost impossible to imagine a person so wicked that he has no conscience left. We may stop our ears to the voice of conscience for long periods at a time, but **sooner or later it will speak up**, asking us to reflect on what we have done, or thought. **Jesus will always wait for that moment.**

Here Jesus is telling us a truth about our souls, that part of us which may live for ever in God. **Like a coin, the soul is precious and never loses its value to God.** Seeing this may help us with loving others, particularly when they are not attractive to us. We should love that value which is God's estimation, the value which he sets, seek it out, and also take care of it in ourselves.

26

The Imperative of Love

The Good Samaritan

Luke 10: 25–37

10:25 There was a lawyer who, to disconcert him, stood up and said to him, 'Master, what must I do to inherit eternal life?'

10:26 He said to him, 'What is written in the Law? What do you read there?'

10:27 He replied, 'You must love the Lord your God with all your heart, with all your soul, with all your strength, and with all your mind, and your neighbour as yourself.'

10:28 'You have answered right,' said Jesus 'do this and life is yours.'

10:29 But the man was anxious to justify himself and said to Jesus, 'And who is my neighbour?'

10:30 Jesus replied, 'A man was once on his way down from Jerusalem to Jericho and fell into the hands of brigands; they took all he had, beat him and then made off, leaving him half dead.

10:31 'Now a priest happened to be travelling down the same road, but when he saw the man, he passed by on the other side.

10:32 'In the same way a Levite who came to the place saw him, and passed by on the other side.

10:33 'But a Samaritan traveller who came upon him was moved with compassion when he saw him.

10:34 'He went up and bandaged his wounds, pouring oil and wine on them. He then lifted him on to his own mount, carried him to the inn and looked after him.

10:35 'Next day, he took out two denarii and handed them to the innkeeper. "Look after him," he said "and on my way back I will make good any extra expense you have."

10:36 'Which of these three, do you think, proved himself a neighbour to the man who fell into the brigands' hands?'

10:37 'The one who took pity on him' he replied. Jesus said to him, 'Go, and do the same yourself.'

The lawyer's question was simple: he was probably hoping for an answer which would give him easy instructions for getting to heaven. Jesus disappoints him by making him give the proper answer himself, the one to be found in the Old Testament when God speaks to Moses and Moses later teaches the people of Israel. That answer, Jesus says, is all there is to it. Jesus came not to set aside the Old Law given to the prophets, but to confirm it and to reinforce it with new meaning.

In both the Old Law and in Jesus' teaching, **God the Father comes first. God is the source of all that is good. He is the Creator of the world and we are his creatures.** If we put God at the centre of our lives, we shall see that God wants us to be for *him* in every aspect and department of our living – heart, soul, strength and mind. There is not a place we keep for God, and the rest for ourselves. The more we learn about God, the clearer it becomes that he is saying to us, **'What you want to do for me, I want you to do for other people also – they are mine too.'** 'Love your

neighbour as yourself' (Mark 12:33). **He is the source of all love that is true love.** In our small and individual love, we share in and pass on something from the vastness of his love.

Jesus tells us who our neighbour is. He gives the answer in this parable not long after he and his disciples had passed through a village belonging to the Samaritans. The Samaritans had not welcomed them and they had had to continue on their way. The Samaritans had a separate religion and kept themselves to themselves. They were not popular with other people – hence the real generosity in the Samaritan's behaviour in the parable. He stepped outside the constraints, and indeed the excuses, of the culture of his people and their time. Christ's call to each of us is also radical and is a call for a radical response.

Our neighbour is therefore **anybody at all with whom we have contact**, not just those to whom we owe friendship because of family relationships, nationality, business connection, or any other special link. Our duty to these is already obvious. The New Law of Jesus is that even people we do not know, are loved by God and they are therefore our neighbours in God's love. Moses was teaching the people of Israel; Jesus teaches the world; and the people of the New Israel are all men who hear him. He is proposing a radically new vision of our daily reality.

The Mass stresses this limitlessness of Divine Love which draws into communion the universal Church and works for the saving of all the world.

27

The Father's Unchanging Love

The Prodigal Son

Luke 15: 11–32

15:11 He also said, 'A man had two sons.

15:12 'The younger said to his father, "Father, let me have the share of the estate that would come to me." So the father divided the property between them.

15:13 'A few days later, the younger son got together everything he had and left for a distant country where he squandered his money on a life of debauchery.

15:14 'When he had spent it all, that country experienced a severe famine, and now he began to feel the pinch,

15:15 'so he hired himself out to one of the local inhabitants who put him on his farm to feed the pigs.

15:16 'And he would willingly have filled his belly with the husks the pigs were eating but no one offered him anything.

15:17 'Then he came to his senses and said, "How many of my father's paid servants have more food than they want, and here am I dying of hunger!

15:18 ' "I will leave this place and go to my father and

112

say: Father, I have sinned against heaven and against you;

15:19 ' "I no longer deserve to be called your son; treat me as one of your paid servants."

15:20 'So he left the place and went back to his father. While he was still a long way off, his father saw him and was moved with pity. He ran to the boy, clasped him in his arms and kissed him tenderly.

15:21 'Then his son said, "Father, I have sinned against heaven and against you. I no longer deserve to be called your son."

15:22 'But the father said to his servants, "Quick! Bring out the best robe and put it on him; put a ring on his finger and sandals on his feet.

15:23 ' "Bring the calf we have been fattening, and kill it; we are going to have a feast, a celebration,

15:24 ' "because this son of mine was dead and has come back to life; he was lost and is found." And they began to celebrate.

15:25 'Now the elder son was out in the fields and on his way back, as he drew near the house, he could hear music and dancing.

15:26 'Calling one of the servants he asked what it was all about.

15:27 ' "Your brother has come" replied the servant "and your father has killed the calf we had fattened because he has got him back safe and sound."

15:28 'He was angry then and refused to go in, and his father came out to plead with him;

15:29 'but he answered his father, "Look, all these years I have slaved for you and never once disobeyed your orders, yet you never offered me so much as a kid for me to celebrate with my friends.

15:30 ' "But, for this son of yours, when he comes back after swallowing up your property – he and his women – you kill the calf we had been fattening."

15:31 'The father said, "My son, you are with me always and all I have is yours.

15:32 ' "But it was only right we should celebrate and rejoice, because your brother here was dead and has come to life; he was lost and is found." '

Jesus often speaks of sinners and forgiveness of sins. In this parable he gives us **an image of a sinner and our Father in heaven who accepts all who turn towards him.**

The first part of the parable describes the son's dreadful behaviour; how he falls very low; how his thoughtless and loose living have brought him no happiness. **He knows he would be better off as one of his father's servants.** This is not, however, a cynical calculation; **he recognises his sins and he is genuinely sorry about them. By wanting to step away from the sins he can see, he does not expect to escape some of their consequences** – he is prepared to work as one of the servants – **but he removes that barrier to receiving his father's love. His father has always loved him, but his father's love could not reach him while he was still caught up with himself.**

The second part is about the brother who stayed at home. It is hard not to feel some sympathy for him. The prodigal son gets a reception which he never had, despite his loyalty and hard work. By our standards there may seem to be some inequity in their treatment. And that is Jesus' point: we know our own standards well enough and find them comforting, but we are to live by God's. They are different from ours. **By God's standard, the brother's love falls short. Love does not harbour to itself, does not desire for itself, does not covet. If God were to say to us, 'You are always with me, and all that is mine is yours',** what would we not give up and suffer to let that be true? **Jesus' message is that this is just what God is actually saying to us. This is also what communion means.**

114

This parable shows us two sides of ourselves: we tend to be glad we are not as bad as the prodigal son and then feel sorry for the brother who has been good. But the brother is also selfish and in his selfishness he is like the other who ran off. **We are in ourselves both prodigal sons and selfish stay-at-homes. The unchanging figure in the story is the father** who is **open in his love and generous with his children.** It takes us time to realise how good our Father in heaven is; it is harder to believe this than we like to think. If we ask God the Father for faith and hope, we are already, like the prodigal son, making a start and are on the way home.

28

Healing in the Spirit

Jesus Heals the Paralytic

Mark 2: 1–12

2:1   When he returned to Capernaum some time later, word went round that he was back;

2:2   and so many people collected that there was no room left, even in front of the door. He was preaching the word to them

2:3   when some people came bringing him a paralytic carried by four men,

2:4   but as the crowd made it impossible to get the man to him, they stripped the roof over the place where Jesus was; and when they had made an opening, they lowered the stretcher on which the paralytic lay.

2:5   Seeing their faith, Jesus said to the paralytic, 'My child, your sins are forgiven.'

2:6   Now some scribes were sitting there, and they thought to themselves,

2:7   'How can this man talk like that? He is blaspheming. Who can forgive sins but God?'

2:8   Jesus, inwardly aware that this was what they were thinking, said to them, 'Why do you have these thoughts in your hearts?

2:9   'Which of these is easier: to say to the paralytic, "Your sins are forgiven" or to say, "Get up, pick up your stretcher and walk"?

2:10 'But to prove to you that the Son of man has authority on earth to forgive sins,' –

2:11 he said to the paralytic – 'I order you: get up, pick up your stretcher, and go off home.'

2:12 And the man got up, picked up his stretcher at once and walked out in front of everyone, so that they were all astounded and praised God saying, 'We have never seen anything like this'.

Once people know where Jesus is, they gather round him in crowds. Some come with faith and some without it. His patience with the crowds is a lesson in itself.

The four men who bring the paralysed man have faith. They think that Jesus will heal their friend and make tremendous efforts to get him close to Jesus. We may wonder if they were not a little surprised when Jesus said to the paralysed man, 'Your sins are forgiven'.

This gives those who do not believe in Jesus their chance. The scribes were learned men who taught and interpreted the religious Law (the Torah). Here they are an image of the self-importance of the world and attachment to the status quo. They think that Jesus' forgiving the man his sins is an insult to religion. Who can forgive sin, but God alone? They are indifferent to Jesus' point that **it is sin, not sickness, which comes between man and God** and is the barrier which must be removed.

Jesus calls himself the Son of man. We know Jesus as the Son of God, brought into the world with messages of angels; **The Son of man is a title which reminds us that he is also completely human and, like us, subject to his**

117

Father. The humanity of Christ is a mystery and we must ask God for help with it. Jesus was completely human and yet without sin. Is the true humanity to which we are called, perhaps only realisable in our life after death, a life without sin? It bears reflection on how we react to the proposal that we should try to imitate Christ in our own living. 'That's not for me – for saints perhaps, but not for me' is a natural reaction, often argued with genuine humility. But it is a reaction which avoids looking at that horizon of eternity from which Christ calls us. It avoids the risks we should have to run with ourselves, if we really tried to answer the call. It sticks to a policy of safety first, by the standards of the world. It illuminates our lack of faith.

Is it not the Church which brings us close to Jesus, like the men who carried their friend the paralytic? We are sometimes held down, almost paralysed, by our lack of faith. **Others take us to Jesus with their faith. Their part in healing us is their sharing in the work of Jesus today.** We usually do not see this. **Jesus is helping us whether we are looking or not.**

Jesus' understanding of our weakness is shown in his juxtaposing the issues of sin and sickness. The sin he addresses in the Gospels is often original sin, rather than grave personal sin. Our situation is original sin. Does he see our weakness in this situation as almost akin to sickness, like that of someone in the grip of disease, potentially well, but too weak to be well of his or her own accord? In calling us out of the world to the spirit, is he showing us the dimension on which we may meet our cure? In defeating death by his sacrifice, he shows us the road across the world which must die, to a new life.

The healed paralytic who carries his stretcher home gives us an insight into the action of the sacraments. His walking is a bodily manifestation of a cure, a grace, which is interior and spiritual. Jesus does not neglect daily physical needs and teaches us to pray for them in the Our Father (Luke 11:2–4), but his main concern is with the life of souls to be saved in a different way. What second thoughts, therefore, we always need when we are tempted to judge others' sins, especially those of the children.

29

The Unity of Christ

The Bread of Life

John 6: 28–36

6:28   Then they said to him, 'What must we do if we are to do the works that God wants?'

6:29   Jesus gave them this answer, 'This is working for God: you must believe in the one he has sent.'

6:30   So they said, 'What sign will you give to show us that we should believe in you? What work will you do?

6:31   'Our fathers had manna to eat in the desert; as scripture says: He gave them bread from heaven to eat.'

6:32   Jesus answered: 'I tell you most solemnly, it was not Moses who gave you bread from heaven, it is my Father who gives you the bread from heaven, the true bread;

6:33   'for the bread of God is that which comes down from heaven and gives life to the world.'

6:34   'Sir,' they said 'give us that bread always.'

6:35   Jesus answered: 'I am the bread of life. He who comes to me will never be hungry; he who believes in me will never thirst.

6:36   'But, as I have told you, you can see me and still you do not believe.'

6:41 Meanwhile the Jews were complaining to each other about him, because he had said, 'I am the bread that came down from heaven.'

6:42 'Surely this is Jesus son of Joseph' they said. 'We know his father and mother. How can he now say, "I have come down from heaven"?'

6:43 Jesus said in reply, 'Stop complaining to each other.

6:44 'No one can come to me unless he is drawn by the Father who sent me, and I will raise him up at the last day.

6:45 'It is written in the prophets: They will all be taught by God, and to hear the teaching of the Father, and learn from it, is to come to me.

6:46 'Not that anybody has seen the Father, except the one who comes from God: he has seen the Father.

6:47 'I tell you most solemnly, everybody who believes has eternal life.

6:48 'I am the bread of life.

6:49 'Your fathers ate the manna in the desert and they are dead;

6:50 'but this is the bread that comes down from heaven, so that a man may eat it and not die.

6:51 'I am the living bread which has come down from heaven. Anyone who eats this bread will live for ever; and the bread that I shall give is my flesh, for the life of the world.'

6:52 Then the Jews started arguing with one another: 'How can this man give us his flesh to eat?' they said.

6:53 Jesus replied: 'I tell you most solemnly, if you do not eat the flesh of the Son of man and drink his blood, you will not have life in you.

6:54 'Anyone who does eat my flesh and drink my blood has eternal life, and I shall raise him up on the last day.

6:55 'For my flesh is real food and my blood is real drink.

6:56 'He who eats my flesh and drinks my blood lives in me and I live in him.

6:57 'As I, who am sent by the living Father, myself draw
life from the Father, so whoever eats me will draw life
from me.

6:58 'This is the bread come down from heaven; not like
the bread our ancestors ate: they are dead, but anyone
who eats this bread will live for ever.'

This passage comes soon after the feeding of the five thousand.
Jesus takes his teaching to a new level of language. He
explicitly says that **he is the Bread of Life.**

Jesus' introduction is quite clear. He states that the work of
God which we are to do, is to have faith: 'to believe in him
whom he has sent.' And which of us could have conceived
of the same answer? We find it easier to focus on works we
can complete today, where we can be the achievers, the win-
ners. It is so easy to forget that these 'horizontal' works in the
world derive their validity entirely from the vertical relationship of faith.

And then, as if there could be any doubt about faith truly
being a work which exerts us (the people were after another
'horizontal' miracle like the feeding of the five thousand),
**Jesus makes his statement 'I am the Bread of Life . . .
which comes down from heaven.'**

The resonances and associations of the language Jesus uses
are immediate to his Jewish listeners. The bread from heav-
en, the Manna, is for them still a vivid image as is also Elijah,
saved on his long journey through the desert by the food
brought him by the angel. But how are these memories to
be personified in Jesus? Here indeed is a need for faith. And
if that is not tough enough, Jesus takes us a stage further:
'The bread which I shall give for the life of the world is my
flesh.' At once we are put into the context of sacrifice and
we recall the suffering servant in Isaiah, the sacrificial victim,
the sacrifice of Abraham, his readiness to offer his son to God
and the ram God sent. The Jews would remember the lambs

used for the Passover sacrifice and some of those present would remember how John the Baptist had greeted Jesus when he first met him, as 'the Lamb of God'. But perhaps some did not and they would have been shocked and confused, rejecting quickly what they could not understand. How natural that impatient defensiveness is. What trust and nerve we need to lay aside the security of the confidence which comes of 'I know best'. This challenge to be open to those around us and to the presence of divine mysteries in our lives still confronts us.

Jesus brings together two major themes in the Old Testament: the Word, the action of God in creating and giving life to the world (God said, 'Let there be light' – Genesis 1:3), and the drama of the imperfect response of fallen humankind to the Word in gratitude, love and sacrifice. The depth of the brief statement in John's prologue to his Gospel is opened up for us: 'The Word became flesh, he lived among us' (John 1:14). The incarnate God directly addresses us. The Word, living among us, leads us towards the perfect response to the Father who utters the Word.

The communion meal of the Mass rehearses this unity which is Jesus. The liturgy of the Word draws together the revealed teaching and prayer from the narrative and psalms of the Old Testament, and their fulfilment in the Gospel of Jesus. At the Offertory, we in our gift offerings participate in our own sacrifice of praise and thanksgiving. We bring the bread and wine, the 'work of human hands', returning to God the gift of life in this world which he has given to us. In the Liturgy of the Eucharist, Jesus, the Word incarnate, makes his once and for all – eternally present in the Eucharist and perfect – sacrifice to the Father and gives us the food of the spirit which gives us life in eternity in God. The priest gives us this sacrament by performing its outward signs. The inner grace is God's.

30

A Deep Faith

The Centurion's Servant

Luke 7: 1–10

7:1 When he had come to the end of all he wanted the people to hear, he went into Capernaum.

7:2 A centurion there had a servant, a favourite of his, who was sick and near death.

7:3 Having heard about Jesus he sent some Jewish elders to him to ask him to come and heal his servant.

7:4 When they came to Jesus they pleaded earnestly with him. 'He deserves this of you' they said

7:5 'because he is friendly towards our people; in fact, he is the one who built the synagogue.'

7:6 So Jesus went with them, and was not very far from the house when the centurion sent word to him by some friends: 'Sir,' he said 'do not put yourself to trouble; because I am not worthy to have you under my roof;

7:7 'and for this same reason I did not presume to come to you myself; but give the word and let my servant be cured.

7:8 'For I am under authority myself, and have soldiers

124

under me; and I say to one man: Go, and he goes; to another: Come here, and he comes; to my servant: Do this, and he does it.'

7:9   When Jesus heard these words he was astonished at him and, turning round, said to the crowd following him, 'I tell you, not even in Israel have I found faith like this.'

7:10   And when the messengers got back to the house they found the servant in perfect health.

This account of Jesus' healing the centurion's servant puts light into the dark, difficult topic of faith. **The centurion**, a foreigner among the Jews, is a model for us gentiles. **He has given us the last words we used to say at Mass before taking Holy Communion, 'Lord, I am not worthy that you should enter under my roof. Say but the word and I shall be healed.'**

Luke gives a good account of this Roman soldier: he is kind to his servant and he has a good name among the Jews. They tell Jesus that he has built them a synagogue. They recommend him to our Lord. This sympathetic man must have heard people discussing Jesus, but we do not know why he should have reached the personal conclusion that Jesus could exercise divine power and heal the servant. This, however, is the stand he takes in asking Jesus' help. He seems to have a deep insight into the mission of Christ. **He makes an analogy between his own authority in Palestine which the imperial power of distant Rome gives him, and the authority which Jesus on earth has from his Father in heaven.** We do not know if the centurion saw that Jesus was God incarnate, but he understands that behind the person of Jesus stands a greater power which he cannot see. **If seeing is believing, believing without seeing is faith.**

This looking beyond the experience of life, this putting confidence in the God who cannot be seen, is the 'work of faith' to which Jesus called the people after the feeding of the five thousand. Faith has never 'made it'. It endures, trusting in what, in this life, it cannot attain. Whatever it does attain, it knows is not the true object of its trust. Faith accepts as the true reality that mystery which it cannot put to the test. Hence the centurion in Luke's version does not even meet Jesus. **He simply sends a message in which he makes clear his trust: he is convinced that power, like his own, will be given to Jesus from above.** He is not looking at Jesus as a source of miraculous benefits which he may use. Through Jesus he implicitly addresses the Father, trusting that Jesus is able to mediate the Father's absolute power. **His faith is not contingent on Jesus' personality and miracles. His faith is set on the eternal God.**

In Matthew's version, the centurion does meet Jesus and Jesus' comment on the man's faith is fuller: 'In truth I tell you, in no one in Israel have I found faith as great as this. And I tell you that many will come from East and West and sit at table with Abraham and Isaac and Jacob at the feast in the kingdom of Heaven; but the children of the kingdom will be thrown out into the darkness outside where there will be weeping and gnashing of teeth' (Matthew 8:10–12). These words are taken to be about the gentiles who will come to believe in Jesus.

The Romans were gentiles and so are we. Jesus, sharing our nature, sees how difficult faith is for us. He holds up across the centuries the model of this foreign soldier from whom we may learn 'the work of God'. Let us assent, make an offering of ourselves, to the gift of faith as did that other centurion who was at the crucifixion and 'had seen how he had died, and said, "In truth, this man was Son of God"' (Mark 15:38–39).'

31

A Kingdom of Love

The Kingdom of Heaven

Matthew 13: 44–52

Parables of the treasure and of the pearl

13:44 'The kingdom of heaven is like treasure hidden in a
field which someone has found; he hides it again, goes
off happy, sells everything he owns and buys the field.
13:45 'Again, the kingdom of heaven is like a merchant
looking for fine pearls;
13:46 'when he finds one of great value he goes and sells
everything he owns and buys it.

Parable of the dragnet

13:47 'Again, the kingdom of heaven is like a dragnet cast
into the sea that brings in a haul of all kinds.
13:48 'When it is full, the fishermen haul it ashore; then, sitting down, they collect the good ones in a basket and
throw away those that are no use.

13:49 'This is how it will be at the end of time: the angels will appear and separate the wicked from the just

13:50 'to throw them into the blazing furnace where there will be weeping and grinding of teeth.

13:51 'Have you understood all this?' They said, 'Yes'.

13:52 And he said to them, 'Well then, every scribe who becomes a disciple of the kingdom of heaven is like a householder who brings out from his storeroom things both new and old.'

What is the kingdom of heaven and what is it like? Jesus gives us three images to help us.

Firstly, the heaven of which we can have an idea which we carry with us through our everyday lives, Jesus likens to **a treasure which is a secret for the man who finds it.** So much does the man want it that **he sells everything else until he has enough money to buy the place where he has left the treasure hidden. A glimpse of heaven, or a touch from God in our lives, has an effect** on us. But the effect is not to feel holy and specially good, it is to *be* a bit holier – **we do good. We 'sell', let go, the things we are fond of which prevent us getting closer to God.** This is virtue and the road to heaven, actually doing the right thing, and not just thinking about it, dying to the world, to our attachments which are not to God and his Word in creation.

Similarly, the pearl merchant: he was dealing with good and precious things all the time, but then finds **something so much more precious and beautiful that he gives up all else.**

The last image is of the very doors of heaven, our deaths. Jesus tells us that **we cannot expect to be able to choose at the last moment. We can be sure that we shall go to God as we really are, and not as we would choose**

to present ourselves. When on the last day, the angels draw in the nets and sort out the fish which are the souls of the dead, they will be able to tell which are the good ones. We have to prepare now.

The first two images tell us that the kingdom is also present, if hidden, or not yet found, in our world. The distinction between the world which is God's creation and the setting he intends for us, and the world to which we should die, is a moral distinction. As in reading the Ten Commandments, we give priority over prohibitions to an active search for God's will of love. *Ubi caritas et amor, ibi Deus est*: where there is charity and love, there is God. God's kingdom is in the spirit and is love.

So Jesus explains those intimations which we occasionally get in life of a world beyond time. The mystery is that that world is both utterly separate and yet immediate to us in our world of time. The kingdom of God is where God's holiness is supreme. The question is whether we can recognise it, or even allow that it should be so. At Mass, we are present at the sacrifice performed by the priest and also present at the once and for all, but eternal sacrifice of Jesus.

The last passage says something about hell. Hell is no less baffling than the idea of heaven. It does not help us much to think a lot about hell. Better thinking about God, not a world without him. We should remember that our souls do not have to go to God. It is up to God's mercy. Jesus teaches that God's mercy is there for all who seek it, in faith and true repentance for sin.

Now is a good time to start. A child preparing for first confession and for first Holy Communion can make a daily examination of conscience a special part of this preparation in this way. At the end of each day, think what are the things which I would be sorry for or ashamed of, if I were actually talking to Jesus face to face. I count them to myself and say that I am sorry. Then I count the things I have done which have cost me effort, patience, or kindness, occasions when I have tried to help. For each of these, I put a grain of wheat into a wine glass. I keep adding to them every night. These grains, each representing its own event, can be the offering I make to Jesus. Just before first Holy Communion, they can be made into the hosts which the priest will consecrate at that Mass. There are a number of religious orders which make communion hosts and one of them will be sure to help out with this special request.

32

Jesus Appoints Peter

The First Warning and Jesus Founds the Church

Matthew 16: 13–27

16:13 When Jesus came to the region of Caesarea Philippi he put this question to his disciples, 'Who do people say the Son of man is?'

16:14 And they said, 'Some say he is John the Baptist, some Elijah, and others Jeremiah or one of the prophets.'

16:15 'But you,' he said 'who do you say I am?'

16:16 Then Simon Peter spoke up, 'You are the Christ,' he said 'the Son of the living God.'

16:17 Jesus replied, 'Simon son of Jonah, you are a happy man! Because it was not flesh and blood that revealed this to you but my Father in heaven.

16:18 'So I now say to you: You are Peter and on this rock I will build my Church. And the gates of the underworld can never hold out against it.

16:19 'I will give you the keys of the kingdom of heaven: whatever you bind on earth shall be considered bound in heaven; whatever you loose on earth shall be considered loosed in heaven.'

16:20 Then he gave the disciples strict orders not to tell anyone that he was the Christ.

16:21 From that time Jesus began to make it clear to his disciples that he was destined to go to Jerusalem and suffer grievously at the hands of the elders and chief priests and scribes, to be put to death and to be raised up on the third day.

16:22 Then, taking him aside, Peter started to remonstrate with him. 'Heaven preserve you, Lord;' he said 'this must not happen to you.'

16:23 But he turned and said to Peter, 'Get behind me, Satan! You are an obstacle in my path, because the way you think is not God's way but man's.'

16:24 Then Jesus said to his disciples, 'If anyone wants to be a follower of mine, let him renounce himself and take up his cross and follow me.

16:25 'For anyone who wants to save his life will lose it; but anyone who loses his life for my sake will find it.

16:26 'What, then, will a man gain, if he wins the whole world and ruins his life? Or what has a man to offer in exchange for his life?

16:27 'For the Son of man is going to come in the glory of his Father with his angels, and, when he does, he will reward each one according to his behaviour.'

Jesus' question to his disciples reveals that in spite of the miracles and his teaching, many people still do not believe that he is the Son of God. They think that he is John the Baptist or one of the prophets come back to life. Peter, however, is growing in faith. He believes in Jesus and Jesus tells him that his faith makes him blessed, close to God. **Faith is a gift from God.**

Then playing on Peter's name (PETRA means a rock in Greek), Jesus tells Peter he is the rock on which he, Jesus, will build his Church. Death, Jesus says, will have no power over his Church; that **what Peter does will be as though it were done in heaven.**

Peter can surely have had little idea what Jesus was talking about. The word 'church' at that time meant a gathering or assembly of the people. There were no churches as we know them, only synagogues, the Temple in Jerusalem and the temples of the pagans. And Jesus' followers were not formally organised, like a club or society. His disciples went everywhere with him. How should they not? **Nobody had thought that Jesus would go away. They were soon to learn that he would be going.** On earth, Jesus says, Peter will stand in his place. **The people of God on earth, the Church, will have Peter, as a building has the ground it stands on.**

Jesus then tells the disciples that he must suffer at the hands of the priests of the temple and the scribes, that he will be killed and rise from the dead on the third day. Peter does not seem to hear the last bit, and is angry. How could God let his son be killed? Jesus in turn seems exasperated. Peter has missed the point.

Jesus explains. **Life**, that thing we fear most to lose, **can only last forever with God.** We have the power to choose, even if in the pressure of our daily lives, it scarcely seems like it. If our choice is for God's will of love, rather than our own, we make a strategic choice of direction. The tactical implications will be hard. So much will seem to be going wrong. There will be many crises which will make us feel lonely. For the few, the crisis will mean the loss of life itself. For most of us, the consequences of our infidelity to that strategic choice will seem manageable, apparently worth it at the time, as Peter was to find out later. The image of the great sacrifices made by the martyrs may remind us of the scale of what is at stake in our blander lives. The more we reflect on and are sensitive to the implications of our choice, the more we shall see the shape of the cross which stands at the heart of each existence. Jesus here points to that cross and asks us to follow him.

133

33

Love Which Accepts Death

The Second Warning and 'Who is the Greatest?'

Mark 9: 30–37

9:30   After leaving that place they made their way through Galilee; and he did not want anyone to know,

9:31   because he was instructing his disciples; he was telling them, 'The Son of man will be delivered into the hands of men; they will put him to death; and three days after he has been put to death he will rise again.'

9:32   But they did not understand what he said and were afraid to ask him.

9:33   They came to Capernaum, and when he was in the house he asked them, 'What were you arguing about on the road?'

9:34   They said nothing because they had been arguing which of them was the greatest.

9:35   So he sat down, called the Twelve to him and said, 'If anyone wants to be first, he must make himself last of all and servant of all.'

9:36   He then took a little child, set him in front of them, put his arms round him, and said to them,

9:37 'Anyone who welcomes one of these little children in my name, welcomes me; and anyone who welcomes me welcomes not me but the one who sent me.'

When Jesus again warns his disciples that he will be killed and rise on the third day, again they do not fully understand him. In one way we understand better because we know what happened later. In another way, it is just as difficult for us to understand.

All that the disciples had learned about Jesus showed that he was good and used his power to help people. He had great love for those he met. He spoke constantly about God, his Father in heaven. They believed that Jesus was the Son of God. Like Martha, perhaps they could say with conviction, 'Yes, Master, I have believed that you are the Messiah, the Son of God, who was to come into the world' (John 11:27). Perhaps nonetheless it would have been hard for them to say what exactly they meant by this. The identification of Jesus with the mysterious person foretold in the Old Testament might in some way explain his goodness and the supernatural powers he sometimes revealed in his miracles. But the disciples' reaction of uncertainty and puzzlement to what Jesus has to say here shows that, even if they made this connection, they were taking things day by day. Of course so – they did not yet have the full story and hearing something of it in advance, they were confused. How could Jesus be killed? Had he not come into the world to save it, not to be destroyed by it?

Jesus' questioning the disciples about their conversation on the road, leads them further into the mystery of divine love. **The question is not who is to be better or greatest – in this world or in the next.** God's saving the world is not to be a matter of inaugurating a new situation for us in which we shall feel better off than we were before. **God's love does**

not worry about the self, only about loving others more. Therefore, **Jesus says to his disciples, putting others first is the point.** Can we do this, as a radical reorientation, a conversion of our attitudes towards others? **Can we see that as God is utterly concerned with loving his creatures, even the least of them in our eyes, so in loving them, we are loving him,** not because we know him so well that we can easily say that we love him, but because in this love of another we enter into his own attitude of love? Our communion with him in this attitude is itself an act of love. Rather than ranks, classes or orders, the state to which God is calling us is union with him.

Jesus, close to the end of his earthly life, **is pointing more urgently at God** and his holy nature, at the way to understand the meaning of his own death: a being for others to the point of emptying the self for others.

Jesus, in pointing to his own fate, is expressing his total conformity with the will and being of the Father. The Son, Second Person of the Holy Trinity, 'did not cling to his equality with God, but emptied himself to assume the condition of a slave and became as men are; and being as all men are, he was humbler yet, even to accepting death, death on a cross' (Philippians 2:6–8).

Paradox is the optic through which we can get a glimpse of holiness. The disciples have a conversation about which of them is the greatest; Jesus speaks of the one who is last, the servant of all, being first. We pause in the face of the mysterious paradox of our human weakness and our faith that God will fill our emptiness with himself, with his Love which in turn flows outwards to those around us. This ceaseless and inspiring action of love is the Holy Spirit's, the Third Person of the Trinity who moves us, through the Son, to the Father. 'Through him, with him, in him, in the unity of the

136

Holy Spirit, all glory and honour is yours, Almighty Father'. These are the words of the Great Doxology which ends the canon of the Mass. They rehearse our relationship with Jesus, our relationship with the Persons of the Holy Trinity, with our God.

34

Death Which Leads to Life

The Third Warning

Mark 10: 32–34

10:32 They were on the road, going up to Jerusalem; Jesus
was walking on ahead of them; they were in a daze,
and those who followed were apprehensive. Once
more taking the Twelve aside he began to tell them
what was going to happen to him:

10:33 'Now we are going up to Jerusalem, and the Son of
man is about to be handed over to the chief priests
and the scribes. They will condemn him to death and
will hand him over to the pagans,

10:34 'who will mock him and spit at him and scourge him
and put him to death; and after three days he will rise
again.'

A third time Jesus tells the disciples what is to happen to
him. **Now he is actually approaching Jerusalem to celebrate the feast of the Passover.** From his ministry in the
countryside and the small towns of Palestine, **Jesus now
goes up to the great city of God and its temple. Jesus**

says that this encounter with the greatest in the land will lead to his death. They will reject him and destroy him.

In each of his warnings, **he also mentions his 'rising on the third day'.** As we see later in the accounts of the resurrection, the disciples just could not know what this meant.

We believe that Mark's account of the life of Jesus drew heavily on what he heard from Peter. Peter would have been present at this scene. The sense of nervousness and fear in those who were following is vivid – fear of the unknown ahead. And what a powerful form of fear that is. For us, however, and for a child, the passion of the Lord should be inseparable from the fact of Easter, God's victory of love.

35

The Holy of Holies Opened: A New House Built

The Householder and his Vineyard

Matthew 21: 33–42

21:33 'Listen to another parable. There was a man, a landowner, who planted a vineyard; he fenced it round, dug a winepress in it and built a tower; then he leased it to tenants and went abroad.

21:34 'When vintage time drew near he sent his servants to the tenants to collect his produce.

21:35 'But the tenants seized his servants, thrashed one, killed another and stoned a third.

21:36 'Next he sent some more servants, this time a larger number, and they dealt with them in the same way.

21:37 'Finally he sent his son to them. "They will respect my son" he said.

21:38 'But when the tenants saw the son, they said to each other, "This is the heir. Come on, let us kill him and take over his inheritance."

21:39 'So they seized him and threw him out of the vineyard and killed him.

21:40 'Now when the owner of the vineyard comes, what will he do to those tenants?'

21:41 They answered, 'He will bring those wretches to a wretched end and lease the vineyard to other tenants who will deliver the produce to him when the season arrives.'

21:42 Jesus said to them, 'Have you never read in the scriptures: It was the stone rejected by the builders that became the keystone. This was the Lord's doing and it is wonderful to see?'

Foreseeing his own death, Jesus uses an image from the liturgy for the Feast of Tabernacles which is nearly upon them. Jesus gives this parable in Jerusalem. The parable describes what is about to happen to him; it gives us a way to look at our own lives; and it gives a history of the world.

We may understand that **the householder is God and the carefully made vineyard is the land of Israel. The tenants are the people of Israel. The fruits which the householder sends for are the praise and righteous living which the people of God need to give to God.**

The servants are the prophets whom God has sent from time to time to tell the people of Israel to turn to God. **The householder's son is Jesus himself.** The owner of the vineyard's return is the Last Day when we shall all be judged for the lives we have led.

Foreseeing his own death, Jesus recalls the words of Psalm 118, one of the Psalms (113–118) recited at major feasts, like the Passover. It is itself a Psalm associated with the entrance of the people of Israel as they process into the Temple for the Feast of Shelters. This major feast has many themes – celebration ending on the eighth day, the drawing in of the harvest, meals, procession with palm leaves and other greenery – which resonate with the coming events which we now celebrate in Holy Week. The image Jesus borrows from the psalm is of masons choosing stones as they build a house. **The corner stone** is especially important as it **has to complete two walls and support the roof. Jesus is that stone which they rejected:** he is scorned by the world and put to death; but then **that stone is now put as the cornerstone of the new house.** And this is God's doing. The people marvel.

Earlier lines from Psalm 118 are striking:

> I shall not die, I shall live
> to recount the great deeds of Yahweh.
> Though Yahweh punished me sternly,
> he has not abandoned me to death.
> Open for me the gates of saving justice,
> I shall go in and thank Yahweh.
> (Psalm 118:17–19)

We also understand the death of Jesus as his going in – his entering the Holy of Holies as our High Priest to secure atonement for the people once and forever after.

In the Jewish sacrificial rite, the Holy of Holies is the third and screened off compartment of the tabernacle, used for the liturgy in the desert, and later represented by the Temple in Jerusalem. Only the priest may enter here, to the place sacred to God. The priestly role of Jesus, as author and victim of the sacrifice, reveals the salvation theme which is paramount in the climax of Easter.

36

The Last Supper

Luke 22: 7–23

22:7 The day of Unleavened Bread came round, the day on which the Passover had to be sacrificed,

22:8 and he sent Peter and John, saying, 'Go and make the preparations for us to eat the Passover.'

22:9 'Where do you want us to prepare it?' they asked.

22:10 'Listen,' he said 'as you go into the city you will meet a man carrying a pitcher of water. Follow him into the house he enters

22:11 'and tell the owner of the house, "The Master has this to say to you: Where is the dining room in which I can eat the Passover with my disciples?"'

22:12 'The man will show you a large upper room furnished with couches. Make the preparations there.'

22:13 They set off and found everything as he had told them, and prepared the Passover.

22:14 When the hour came he took his place at table, and the apostles with him.

22:15 And he said to them, 'I have longed to eat this Passover with you before I suffer;

22:16 'because, I tell you, I shall not eat it again until it is fulfilled in the kingdom of God.'

22:17 Then, taking a cup, he gave thanks and said, 'Take this and share it among you,

22:18 'because from now on, I tell you, I shall not drink wine until the kingdom of God comes.'

The institution of the Eucharist

22:19 Then he took some bread, and when he had given thanks, broke it and gave it to them, saying, 'This is my body which will be given for you; do this as a memorial of me.'
22:20 He did the same with the cup after supper, and said, 'This cup is the new covenant in my blood which will be poured out for you.

The treachery of Judas foretold

22:21 'And yet, here with me on the table is the hand of the man who betrays me.
22:22 'The Son of man does indeed go to his fate even as it has been decreed, but alas for that man by whom he is betrayed!'
22:23 And they began to ask one another which of them it could be who was to do this thing.

Peter's denial and repentance foretold

Luke 22: 31–34

22:31 'Simon, Simon! Satan, you must know, has got his wish to sift you all like wheat;
22:32 'but I have prayed for you, Simon, that your faith may not fail, and once you have recovered, you in your turn must strengthen your brothers.'
22:33 'Lord,' he answered 'I would be ready to go to prison with you, and to death.'
22:34 Jesus replied, 'I tell you, Peter, by the time the cock

crows today you will have denied three times that you know me.'

Jesus and his disciples prepare to celebrate the feast of the Passover. The foreknowledge of Jesus in directing his disciples where to find the room they will use, puts a sharp accent on the supernatural dimension of the drama which is now in train.

Jesus does not explain himself as **he offers the bread and the wine, saying they are his body and his blood. With these words Christ institutes the sacrament of the Eucharist, the Mass.** The disciples may have remembered how Jesus had spoken of himself as the 'Bread of Life' (John 6:35). Perhaps they did not. The meanings present in Jesus' simple words will have unfolded for them when seen through the experience of his passion which was to follow.

Whatever their understanding at the time, **this Last Supper with Jesus became their contact and meeting again with the risen Christ.** As Jesus had asked them, **they repeated his words and his breaking of the bread ever after. He appeared to them as they did so. 'They knew him in the breaking of bread'** (Luke 24: 35).

From this moment, events move quickly. He knows what is to happen and says so. It is salutary to remember that **the man who betrayed Jesus was one of his chosen Twelve.** He was at the Last Supper and knew Jesus well. **The disciples themselves could not work out who it was to be. None of us knows himself or another as Jesus knows us. He is 'closer to our souls than we are to ourselves'.** See what he says here to Peter. Our own path to holiness can only be in keeping our eyes on Jesus, failing and recovering, like Peter, strengthened by Peter and the Church.

In the Gospel of John, Jesus says, 'Now has the Son of man

been glorified, and in him God has been glorified' (John 13:31). The English theologian and commentator on the Gospel of John, John Marsh, comments on this verse as follows:

'This is peculiarly and strongly the Johannine contribution to Christian thought about the death of Jesus. He wants to make it perfectly plain that it was not the case that Jesus died in shame and ignominy and was afterwards restored to honour and glorified, as if the cross were dishonour and shame, and the resurrection for the first time the moment of victory and glory. To John the whole story was the glorification of the Son of man. It begins at the very moment when the Adversary has sent Judas on his fatal errand. And in him God is glorified. What is taking place is not just the settling of a question about the man Jesus, whose death might be seen in a new perspective by a subsequent narrative of his resurrection. The real issue concerns God who has come to man in the form of man in the Person of Jesus Christ. So the real actor in the drama is God himself, and so God will be glorified in the Son, as the Son will glorify the Father.'*

---

* John Marsh (1968) *Saint John: The Penguin New Testament Commentaries*, Penguin Books, Harmondsworth, pp. 495–6.

37

The Passion

The Mount of Olives

Luke 22: 39–71

22:39 He then left to make his way as usual to the Mount of Olives, with the disciples following.

22:40 When they reached the place he said to them, 'Pray not to be put to the test.'

22:41 Then he withdrew from them, about a stone's throw away, and knelt down and prayed.

22:42 'Father,' he said 'if you are willing, take this cup away from me. Nevertheless, let your will be done, not mine.'

22:43 Then an angel appeared to him, coming from heaven to give him strength.

22:44 In his anguish he prayed even more earnestly, and his sweat fell to the ground like great drops of blood.

22:45 When he rose from prayer he went to the disciples and found them sleeping for sheer grief.

22:46 'Why are you asleep?' he said to them. 'Get up and pray not to be put to the test.'

The arrest

22:47 He was still speaking when a number of men appeared,

and at the head of them the man called Judas, one of the Twelve, who went up to Jesus to kiss him.

22:48 Jesus said, 'Judas, are you betraying the Son of man with a kiss?'

22:49 His followers, seeing what was happening, said, 'Lord, shall we use our swords?'

22:50 And one of them struck out at the high priest's servant, and cut off his right ear.

22:51 But at this Jesus spoke. 'Leave off!' he said 'That will do!' And touching the man's ear he healed him.

22:52 Then Jesus spoke to the chief priests and captains of the Temple guard and elders who had come for him. 'Am I a brigand' he said 'that you had to set out with swords and clubs?

22:53 'When I was among you in the Temple day after day you never moved to lay hands on me. But this is your hour; this is the reign of darkness.'

Peter's denials

22:54 They seized him then and led him away, and they took him to the high priest's house. Peter followed at a distance.

22:55 They had lit a fire in the middle of the courtyard and Peter sat down among them,

22:56 and as he was sitting there by the blaze a servant-girl saw him, peered at him, and said, 'This person was with him too.'

22:57 But he denied it. 'Woman,' he said 'I do not know him.'

22:58 Shortly afterwards someone else saw him and said, 'You are another of them.' But Peter replied, 'I am not, my friend.'

22:59 About an hour later another man insisted, saying, 'This fellow was certainly with him. Why, he is a Galilean.'

22:60 'My friend,' said Peter 'I do not know what you are talking about.' At that instant, while he was still speaking, the cock crew,

22:61 and the Lord turned and looked straight at Peter, and Peter remembered what the Lord had said to him, 'Before the cock crows today, you will have disowned me three times.'

22:62 And he went outside and wept bitterly.

Jesus mocked by the guards

22:63 Meanwhile the men who guarded Jesus were mocking and beating him.

22:64 They blindfolded him and questioned him. 'Play the prophet' they said. 'Who hit you then?'

22:65 And they continued heaping insults on him.

Jesus before the Sanhedrin

22:66 When day broke there was a meeting of the elders of the people, attended by the chief priests and scribes. He was brought before their council,

22:67 and they said to him, 'If you are the Christ, tell us.' 'If I tell you,' he replied 'you will not believe me,

22:68 'and if I question you, you will not answer.

22:69 'But from now on, the Son of man will be seated at the right hand of the Power of God.'

22:70 Then they all said, 'So you are the Son of God then?' He answered, 'It is you who say I am.'

22:71 'What need of witnesses have we now?' they said. 'We have heard it for ourselves from his own lips.'

Jesus before Pilate

Luke 23: 1–27

23:1 The whole assembly then rose, and they brought him before Pilate.

149

23:2 They began their accusation by saying, 'We found this man inciting our people to revolt, opposing payment of the tribute to Caesar, and claiming to be Christ, a king.'

23:3 Pilate put to him this question, 'Are you the king of the Jews?' 'It is you who say it' he replied.

23:4 Pilate then said to the chief priests and the crowd, 'I find no case against this man.'

23:5 But they persisted, 'He is inflaming the people with his teaching all over Judaea; it has come all the way from Galilee, where he started, down to here.'

23:6 When Pilate heard this, he asked if the man were a Galilean;

23:7 and finding that he came under Herod's jurisdiction he passed him over to Herod who was also in Jerusalem at that time.

Jesus before Herod

23:8 Herod was delighted to see Jesus; he had heard about him and had been wanting for a long time to set eyes on him; moreover, he was hoping to see some miracle worked by him.

23:9 So he questioned him at some length; but without getting any reply.

23:10 Meanwhile the chief priests and the scribes were there, violently pressing their accusations.

23:11 Then Herod, together with his guards, treated him with contempt and made fun of him; he put a rich cloak on him and sent him back to Pilate.

23:12 And though Herod and Pilate had been enemies before, they were reconciled that same day.

Jesus before Pilate again

23:13 Pilate then summoned the chief priests and the leading men and the people.

23:14 'You brought this man before me' he said 'as a political agitator. Now I have gone into the matter myself in your presence and found no case against the man in respect of all the charges you bring against him.

23:15 'Nor has Herod either, since he has sent him back to us. As you can see, the man has done nothing that deserves death,

23:16 'So I shall have him flogged and then let him go.'

23:18 But as one man they howled, 'Away with him! Give us Barabbas!'

23:19 (This man had been thrown into prison for causing a riot in the city and for murder.)

23:20 Pilate was anxious to set Jesus free and addressed them again,

23:21 but they shouted back, 'Crucify him! Crucify him!'

23:22 And for the third time he spoke to them, 'Why? What harm has this man done? I have found no case against him that deserves death, so I shall have him punished and then let him go.'

23:23 But they kept on shouting at the top of their voices, demanding that he should be crucified. And their shouts were growing louder.

23:24 Pilate then gave his verdict: their demand was to be granted.

23:25 He released the man they asked for, who had been imprisoned for rioting and murder, and handed Jesus over to them to deal with as they pleased.

The way to Calvary

23:26 As they were leading him away they seized on a man, Simon from Cyrene, who was coming in from the country, and made him shoulder the cross and carry it behind Jesus.

23:27 Large numbers of people followed him, and of women too, who mourned and lamented for him.

The Crucifixion

Luke 23: 32–56

23:32 Now with him they were also leading out two other criminals to be executed.

23:33 When they reached the place called The Skull, they crucified him there and the two criminals also, one on the right, the other on the left.

23:34 Jesus said, 'Father, forgive them; they do not know what they are doing.' Then they cast lots to share out his clothing.

The crucified Christ is mocked

23:35 The people stayed there watching him. As for the leaders, they jeered at him. 'He saved others,' they said 'let him save himself if he is the Christ of God, the Chosen One.'

23:36 The soldiers mocked him too, and when they approached to offer him vinegar

23:37 they said, 'If you are the king of the Jews, save yourself.'

23:38 Above him there was an inscription: 'This is the King of the Jews'.

The good thief

23:39 One of the criminals hanging there abused him. 'Are you not the Christ?' he said. 'Save yourself and us as well.'

23:40 But the other spoke up and rebuked him. 'Have you no fear of God at all?' he said. 'You got the same sentence as he did,

23:41 'but in our case we deserved it: we are paying for what we did. But this man has done nothing wrong.

23:42 'Jesus,' he said 'remember me when you come into your kingdom.'

23:43 'Indeed, I promise you,' he replied 'today you will be with me in paradise.'

The death of Jesus

23:44 It was now about the sixth hour and, with the sun eclipsed, a darkness came over the whole land until the ninth hour.

23:45 The veil of the Temple was torn right down the middle;

23:46 and when Jesus had cried out in a loud voice, he said, 'Father, into your hands I commit my spirit.' With these words he breathed his last.

After the death

23:47 When the centurion saw what had taken place, he gave praise to God and said, 'This was a great and good man.'

23:48 And when all the people who had gathered for the spectacle saw what had happened, they went home beating their breasts.

23:49 All his friends stood at a distance; so also did the women who had accompanied him from Galilee, and they saw all this happen.

The burial

23:50 Then a member of the council arrived, an upright and virtuous man named Joseph.

23:51 He had not consented to what the others had planned and carried out. He came from Arimathaea, a Jewish town, and he lived in the hope of seeing the kingdom of God.

23:52 This man went to Pilate and asked for the body of Jesus.

23:53 He then took it down, wrapped it in a shroud and put him in a tomb which was hewn in stone in which no one had yet been laid.

23:54 It was Preparation Day and the sabbath was imminent.

23:55 Meanwhile the women who had come from Galilee with Jesus were following behind. They took note of the tomb and of the position of the body.

23:56 Then they returned and prepared spices and ointments. And on the sabbath day they rested, as the Law required.

If the life of Jesus has been carefully studied, if we have come to think of him as a person we feel we know, this vivid narrative is moving, shocking. Indeed our rational selves and our human feelings of fairness are affronted. Why did all this have to happen? Why did it happen? We are up against what is traditionally known as the 'Folly of the Cross'. Most children see it plainly. We cannot easily evade this problem, nor dispose of it. We have to place ourselves before the teaching of John who records the Lord saying, 'Now has the Son of man been glorified, and in him God has been glorified.'

First, let us try to understand why the **chief priests** wanted Jesus to be killed. They **saw him** and his teaching **as a threat** to their established positions, to the teaching and law which they wanted upheld. They could not expect the Roman governor, Pilate, to understand this clearly so they emphasised that Jesus was a trouble-maker who could upset peace in the province. That, as governor, would touch his interests directly.

Why did Pilate go along with this, when he could find no fault in Jesus? He appears, like Herod faced with Salome's demand for John the Baptist's head, to have been weak. An appalling web of compromise, irresponsibility and short-term advantage is being woven. An enormous crowd is shouting for Barabbas and wanting Jesus executed. Pilate's aim was to keep the province quiet, and to give in to local demands when they did not affect essential Roman interests. Pilate did not consider himself responsible for great matters of religion. **He went along with the local people's demands in order to protect the matters of state he did know about.** What a profoundly contemporary man!

Secondly, why did Jesus, the Son of God, allow himself to be put to death? To save us from our sins. But how? Here we need to remember that main theme in all his teaching, 'Thy will be done.' So we ask our question of the Father. And he does not answer. We sense the immediacy of the mystery of God. Our attempts to resolve, to make sense of this Paschal mystery, the mystery of Christ's own Passover, end ineluctably with our not knowing. The paradox of suffering and salvation is hard. But paradox for the Christian does not lie in an event or an occurrence, but is an essential condition of our humanity. Living in faith, no matter how weakly, we become aware that everything is happening at once and never more vividly than in meditating on the Passion. We find that our faith cannot sort out the paradox, it cannot arrive. It is always drawn to a new horizon. But our striving towards the horizon is in hope and, as we go, both hope and faith are sustained and are brought to a new and deeper life.

Searching for the will of the Father we hold on to what we know: that his will is that love will prevail and bring all people into the perfection of his love. The Dutch theologian, Edward Schillebeeckx, catches at what that love means in practice: 'The silence of God when Jesus hung on the cross is logically on a par with Jesus' choice in rejecting any messianism of power.'*

---

* E. Schillebeeckx (1990) *Church: The Human Story of God*, Crossroads Publishing, New York, N.Y., p. 125.

We can recall the fourth 'Song of the Servant' in Isaiah, 'Ill treated and afflicted, he never opened his mouth' (Isaiah 53:7). We recall the words of Jesus himself: 'The Father loves me, because I lay down my life in order to take it up again. No one takes it from me; I lay it down of my own free will' (John 10:17–18).

In this silence and acceptance of defencelessness, there is sacrifice, no symbolic ritual, but the ultimate giving away which Jesus makes of himself, his life. And in this act he makes plain what has always been, always will be, true. He, the Son of God, forgives the sins which are, in his terrible death, committed against him. All sins, ours and theirs, are committed against him and these too he forgives. He himself taught his disciples about the cosmic dimension of this event in the words the priest also uses at the consecration of the wine . . . 'For this is my blood, the blood of the Covenant, poured out for many for the forgiveness of sins' (Matthew 26:28).

The supernatural circumstances which attend the event also speak out this truth. The veil in the Temple is rent in two. The Holy of Holies which only the high priest may enter at the sacrifice on the Day of Atonement, is laid open (cf. Hebrews 6:19 and 9:7–12). Jesus as the priest of his own supreme sacrifice has by his own death completed the law of the Mosaic rite. The metaphor of the Judaic liturgical tabernacle, the Holy of Holies, is consummated and now redundant. In real life, God incarnate in Jesus opens his kingdom to his people for ever. He does so out of love, in love and by love. The human inevitability of Jesus' conflict with the authority of the Jews and of Pilate derives from the consequences of original sin, the way we all are. The love the Father has for his creation is triumphant in forgiving and Jesus, obedient to this love, in his forgiveness as true man and true God, unites human nature with that divine will of love.

These hard thoughts and our human emotional resistance to them stand like a hedge across our path, unless we see and reflect on the fact of the resurrection. And it is to the resurrection that the child, like St Peter, must hurry without delay.

38

The Resurrection

John 20: 1–18

20:1   It was very early on the first day of the week and still dark, when Mary of Magdala came to the tomb. She saw that the stone had been moved away from the tomb,

20:2   and came running to Simon Peter and the other disciple, the one Jesus loved. 'They have taken the Lord out of the tomb' she said 'and we don't know where they have put him.'

20:3   So Peter set out with the other disciple to go to the tomb.

20:4   They ran together, but the other disciple, running faster than Peter, reached the tomb first;

20:5   he bent down and saw the linen cloths lying on the ground, but did not go in.

20:6   Simon Peter who was following now came up, went right into the tomb, saw the linen cloths on the ground,

20:7   and also the cloth that had been over his head; this was not with the linen cloths but rolled up in a place by itself.

20:8   Then the other disciple who had reached the tomb first also went in; he saw and he believed.

20:9 Till this moment they had failed to understand the teaching of scripture, that he must rise from the dead.

20:10 The disciples then went home again.

The appearance to Mary of Magdala

20:11 Meanwhile Mary stayed outside near the tomb, weeping. Then, still weeping, she stooped to look inside,

20:12 and saw two angels in white sitting where the body of Jesus had been, one at the head, the other at the feet.

20:13 They said, 'Woman, why are you weeping?' 'They have taken my Lord away' she replied 'and I don't know where they have put him.'

20:14 As she said this she turned round and saw Jesus standing there, though she did not recognise him.

20:15 Jesus said, 'Woman, why are you weeping? Who are you looking for?' Supposing him to be the gardener, she said, 'Sir, if you have taken him away, tell me where you have put him, and I will go and remove him'.

20:16 Jesus said, 'Mary!' She knew him then and said to him in Hebrew, 'Rabbuni!' – which means Master.

20:17 Jesus said to her, 'Do not cling to me because I have not yet ascended to the Father. But go and find the brothers, and tell them: I am ascending to my Father and your Father, to my God and your God.'

20:18 So Mary of Magdala went and told the disciples that she had seen the Lord and that he had said these things to her.

We turn from the vastness of the crucifixion, the crowds, the violence, the darkness over the earth and the tearing of the Temple veil, to the intimacy of John's own account of what he saw and heard on the first Easter day.

The theme is much vaster: the defeat of death, the coming true of an inscrutable prophecy that Jesus would die and be

159

raised up again on the third day. We see it not as an abstract idea, but personally, close up through the eyes of John and Mary of Magdala, Jesus' friends. It is a fitting reminder that our vision of God is through Jesus and Jesus is a person who calls us to be his friends, close to him.

John admits that until this moment he had still not fully understood that Jesus, Our Lord, was God. Jesus' resurrection, his coming through death, gives us a certainty. This was no ordinary 'good man', but God come to earth. In one sense, perhaps the disciples had already known this and believed it. But now their knowledge took on a new dimension of confidence and faith. It is the same for us. The resurrection illuminates the Gospels. The Passover supper has become a new Passover; Christ's sacrifice of himself is not rejected; his promises are good. When Jesus says, 'This is my body', it is not then, back in history, but now, for we now know he lives with us still.

It defies our human understanding completely to know what Jesus meant when he said to Mary of Magdala, 'Do not cling to me because I have not yet ascended to the Father.' But we may assume that he said it because Mary very much wanted to cling to him. As do we. We must listen carefully to what he says next: 'Go and find the brothers, and tell them: I am ascending to my Father and your Father, to my God and your God.' Jesus brings us to God, to the Father we share with him in heaven. He does this through his action in the Church where Mary and the brothers and each of us may be with him as one. In this way we can now begin to see around us how his death on the cross has saved, has renewed the world.

39

The Road to Emmaus

Luke 24: 13–35

24:13 That very same day, two of them were on their way to a village called Emmaus, seven miles from Jerusalem,

24:14 and they were talking together about all that had happened.

24:15 Now as they talked this over, Jesus himself came up and walked by their side;

24:16 but something prevented them from recognising him.

24:17 He said to them, 'What matters are you discussing as you walk along?' They stopped short, their faces downcast.

24:18 Then one of them, called Cleopas, answered him, 'You must be the only person staying in Jerusalem who does not know the things that have been happening there these last few days.'

24:19 'What things?' he asked. 'All about Jesus of Nazareth' they answered 'who proved he was a great prophet by the things he said and did in the sight of God and of the whole people;

24:20 'and how our chief priests and our leaders handed him over to be sentenced to death, and had him crucified.

24:21 'Our own hope had been that he would be the one

to set Israel free. And this is not all: two whole days have gone by since it all happened;

24:22 'and some women from our group have astounded us: they went to the tomb in the early morning,

24:23 'and when they did not find the body, they came back to tell us they had seen a vision of angels who declared he was alive.

24:24 'Some of our friends went to the tomb and found everything exactly as the women had reported, but of him they saw nothing.'

24:25 Then he said to them, 'You foolish men! So slow to believe the full message of the prophets!

24:26 'Was it not ordained that the Christ should suffer and so enter into his glory?'

24:27 Then, starting with Moses and going through all the prophets, he explained to them the passages throughout the scriptures that were about himself.

24:28 When they drew near to the village to which they were going, he made as if to go on;

24:29 but they pressed him to stay with them. 'It is nearly evening' they said 'and the day is almost over.' So he went in to stay with them.

24:30 Now while he was with them at table, he took the bread and said the blessing; then he broke it and handed it to them.

24:31 And their eyes were opened and they recognised him; but he had vanished from their sight.

24:32 Then they said to each other, 'Did not our hearts burn within us as he talked to us on the road and explained the scriptures to us?'

24:33 They set out that instant and returned to Jerusalem. There they found the Eleven assembled together with their companions,

24:34 who said to them, 'Yes, it is true. The Lord has risen and has appeared to Simon.'

24:35 Then they told their story of what had happened on the road and how they had recognised him at the breaking of bread.

This passage describes **one of the occasions on which Jesus appeared to his disciples after the resurrection.** The disciples fail to recognise Jesus. Like Peter they had been told by Jesus that he would rise on the third day after his death, but they had not really believed him. So, not surprisingly, they were not looking for Jesus, or expecting him, and they did not recognise him as he walked with them on the road.

On the road Jesus explains to the two disciples that this Jesus of Nazareth was indeed the Christ to whom the prophets looked forward, and who would 'set Israel free'. **Jesus gives us his own assurance about the Old Testament and affirms it as the authentic account of God's preparing the world for the coming of his Son. In the Liturgy of the Word at Mass, the readings from the Old Testament are linked to those from the Gospels** and the whole forms a cycle of instruction which runs for three years.

The disciples only **recognise Jesus in the breaking of the bread.** At the Last Supper, Jesus had said, 'This is my body' and 'This is my blood'. At Emmaus the risen Jesus again directly offers himself to them and they recognise him, though only for a moment, and then he disappears. That moment, however, was enough to make sense of all that had passed before – 'Did not our hearts burn within us as he talked to us on the road . . . ?' **At Holy Communion we too have a direct meeting with Jesus.** Maybe we realise this, maybe we do not. Nonetheless, this encounter does happen, deep in the soul. That is our faith.

Thus we are all on the road to Emmaus. Jesus, risen at the resurrection, is with us whether we can recognise him, see him, or not. **He is actually with us and we meet him in our souls at the breaking of bread at Mass.**

Actually getting ourselves to Mass, 'going to church', is the moment of will which is asked of us. Everything of God's is for us and given. But we have to turn to it. That is the moment of our own freedom. Jesus at Emmaus 'made as if to go on'. He did not press his companions; they pressed him to stay and eat with them. And so they recognised him at the meal. Without the advantage of seeing, we have also to press ourselves – the unending work of faith.

Paul points to the centrality of the sacrifice of Jesus in every aspect of our life in his letter to the Ephesians, **'Try, then, to imitate God as children of his that he loves and follow Christ loving as he loved you**, giving himself in our place' – and here Paul quotes from Exodus (29:18) – 'as a fragrant offering and sacrifice to God' (Ephesians 5:1–2).

This love for each other is how we can 'announce him to the brothers', as Jesus asked Mary to do when he met her in the garden by the Tomb (John 20:17).

40

Sacrifice and Ransom

Matthew 20: 26–28

20:26 This is not to happen among you. No; anyone who
wants to be great among you must be your servant,

20:27 and anyone who wants to be first among you must be
your slave,

20:28 just as the Son of man came not to be served but to
serve, and to give his life as a ransom for many.

1 Peter 1: 18–19

1:18 Remember, the ransom that was paid to free you from
the useless way of life your ancestors handed down
was not paid in anything corruptible, neither in silver
nor gold,

1:19 but in the precious blood of a lamb without spot or
stain, namely Christ;

Letter to the Romans 5: 8–9

5:8 But what proves that God loves us is that Christ died
for us while we were still sinners.

5:9   Having died to make us righteous, is it likely that he would now fail to save us from God's anger?

Letter to the Colossians 2: 14

2:14   He has overridden the Law, and cancelled every record of the debt that we had to pay; he has done away with it by nailing it to the cross;

Letter to the Hebrews 2: 14–15

2:14   Since all the children share the same blood and flesh, he too shared equally in it, so that by his death he could take away all the power of the devil, who had power over death,

2:15   and set free all those who had been held in slavery all their lives by the fear of death.

Here Our Lord and his apostles speak of the effect of his sacrifice which is the liberation of humankind from the hold of sin. Writing after the resurrection, the apostles are able to see, and now proclaim, that **this liberation was the intention, the will, of God himself.**

These passages push us deeper into the meaning of the sacrifice of Jesus and into an understanding of sin and its impact on our relationship with God. But the passages are not easy. What are the dangers?

We should be careful with our thinking about **ransom. The basic idea is of something given to release somebody else from some predicament. Through the free sacrifice of his life, Jesus secures our release from the consequences of our sins.** This is no human transaction, as Peter insists, with some price being demanded. **God**

166

does not exact penalties, does not bargain about sin. Paul, writing to the Romans, **points to the open-handed and unconditional mercy of the Father's saving love.** And this is so difficult for us to grasp. We are so caught up with our human notions of justice. Don't we so often see in the Old Testament people assuming that God will deal with the wrong doers, according to our own standards? Looking again through the optic of the New Testament, recalling Jesus' New Commandment: 'Love one another' (John 13:34), perhaps we can see that what they were trying to express was their own strong sense of the consequences of sin. And what are these? The narrowing of our openness to God, the free and autonomous turning aside from the course sought for us by God, from the way to union with him which he so much desires.

We can recognise this gratuitous work of God in our own lives. Doesn't Jesus himself teach that 'No one is good but God alone' (Mark 10:18)? Why then do we so easily assume for our own credit the good that we do and the good which happens to us? Because our faith is weak. It is the Holy Spirit at work in our daily lives, following and helping our every turn towards the good, enabling and completing it when we are open to his help. If we admit the Spirit into our lives by acknowledging his ceaseless work for and in us, then our thoughts and commissions and omissions away from that good will be plainer to see.

Thus God is ceaselessly active in every human life. He is not a spectator, a detached umpire, calculating points for and against. We are not puny contestants in the hostile arena of life, pathetically inadequate against the demands of virtue made of us. **The virtue is all his. Our delight in the good is his delight. He offers us a share in this, quite without regard to whether we have merited it.** Only Jesus can show us this. So it is nearly impossible for us to say when we have been good. Our selfish, acquisitive motives undermine so much of what we may think we have done well. So many of our apparently finer thoughts are really simply our whistling in the night, consciously or unconsciously cheering ourselves up. But **our sins . . . these are truly our own and conscience tells us so.**

What kind of debt our sins may actually incur we can only imagine with our own notions of justice, of mine and yours and fair deals. There may be clear debts to others which we can try to repay by giving back what we have taken. But to God? How should we repay? Can we be in some transactional equality with God? All we can do with safety is to rely on his mercy; rely, as Paul teaches, on the efficacy of Jesus' sacrifice, itself the ultimate action of love for the world, in conformity with the will of love which is the Father's. **We are here to receive this goodness. It is done for us.** Only by admitting this can we free ourselves from destructive absorption in feelings of guilt, reach a more mature recognition of our true responsibility in exercising our will. The unconditional love God has for us and his work in each of our lives through the Holy Spirit look only for our tentative turning of our will towards his, in recognition and love.

41

Sacrifice and Salvation

Luke 24: 26

24:26 'Was it not ordained that the Christ should suffer and
so enter into his glory?'

1 Corinthians 15:3

15:3 Well then, in the first place, I taught you what I had
been taught myself, namely that Christ died for our
sins, in accordance with the scriptures;

2 Corinthians 5: 14–15

5:14 And this is because the love of Christ overwhelms us
when we reflect that if one man has died for all, then
all men should be dead;
5:15 and the reason he died for all was so that living men
should live no longer for themselves, but for him who
died and was raised to life for them.

Acts of the Apostles 2: 23

2:23 'This man, who was put into your power by the

deliberate intention and foreknowledge of God, you took and had crucified by men outside the Law.'

In the first passage above from Luke, the speaker is the risen Christ himself speaking to the two disciples on their way to Emmaus and before they had recognised him that evening in the breaking of the bread. **The two passages from Paul state that Jesus died on account of our sins and in order to save us. That Jesus' death happened according to the clear purpose of God** is emphasised again by St Peter recorded by St Luke in the Acts of the Apostles.

It is hard to avoid a dark and obscure question: 'Why did God the Father, the God who is Love, plan the sacrifice of his Son in atonement for our sins?' The catechism takes our question head on. It points out (Catechism, 599) that **those who handed Jesus over to death were not 'merely passive role players in a scenario written in advance by God'. They acted out of free will.**

We overlook the responsibility we each carry in the autonomy of our free will. God's love never ceases to respect and allow us this free will. It is an awesome fact in the economy of salvation. **And God, for whom all moments of time are immediately present** (Catechism 600), **arranges for us the possibility of our salvation with all the consequences of these free actions of ours already in mind. In some way it was always known to him that our choices would stray, be against him, that the incarnation into our world of the Absolute Good would end in its rejection.** The Father accepts that and knows that the Truth to which he calls us can be served even by that rejection because it is of that Truth which endures for ever that **true love endures even rejection.** Rejection can reveal this further fidelity of love.

A parent sees this in enduring the waywardness and rejections thrown at parents by the children. And this endurance is

170

sacrificial, affirming the bonds of love, the communion which is the life of a family. And so Jesus, utterly at one with the mind of the Father, does not invoke, nor does the Father propose or provide a defensive retaliation, a Messianic intervention of power to ward off death.

Jesus transforms the ghastly violence and cruelty of his Passion into his own act of loving sacrifice: the victim is at once the author and priest of the sacrifice. As priest, his sacrifice is made on behalf of the people, on behalf of us: the God made man acts for all humanity. As this sacrifice also affirms love, it is a celebration of love. Love is glorified. The cross symbolises this supreme moment. Therefore we kiss the wood of the crucifix in the Good Friday liturgy. The cross is the immediate symbol of our faith and our Christian religion.

Paul makes explicit the completion of what was foreshadowed in the experience of Abraham, 'he did not spare his own Son, but gave him up for the sake of us all' (Romans 8:32).

John, who was present at the crucifixion at Calvary, emphasises in his first letter that **love is the key in understanding God's plan of salvation: 'This is the revelation of God's love for us, that God sent his only Son into the world that we may have life through him. Love consists in this: it is not we who loved God, but God loved us first and sent his Son to expiate our sins'** (1 John 4:9–10).

That God's plan to save us would be expressed as sacrifice was prefigured throughout the Old Testament. The people of Israel are taught by the prophets to re-examine their own notions of sacrifice and they learn, guided by the Holy Spirit, to see that in Jesus was the perfection of sacrifice. The imagery may not be so accessible to us because we do not have analogies with our own religious customs, as did the pre-Christians. We do not sacrifice oxen and doves. We have to be told that blood is life. We do not see it as 'fact' on the sacrificial altar. Instead, faithful to Jesus' teaching at the Last Supper, 'Do this in remembrance of me' (Luke 22:19), **we celebrate the perfect sacrifice when, as we believe, Jesus offers it at the Mass**, occurring once only in time on Calvary, eternally present ('This cup is the new Covenant in my blood', Luke 22:20) in the sacramental reality of the Mass.

The 'how' and 'in what way' the life, passion and death of Jesus achieve our salvation remain a mystery of faith, as we proclaim after the consecration at Mass, **'By your death and resurrection, you have set us free. You are the saviour of the world.'** But we can draw closer to the mystery.

The Passion of Jesus establishes a new covenant, a new bond given by God to his people. The Covenant of God's promise given on stone tablets to Moses, is completed in the New Covenant sealed in the blood of Jesus: 'This is my blood, the blood of the covenant, poured out for many' (Mark 14:24) and 'What you have come to is . . . Jesus, the mediator of a new covenant, and to purifying blood which pleads more insistently than Abel's' (Hebrews 12:23–24).

In his making of the supreme sacrifice, mediating the New Covenant, the priesthood of Jesus is perfect. The writer of the Letter to the Hebrews recalls the 'type' of that ancient and obscure figure in Genesis, Melchizedech (Hebrews 6:20) who greeted the triumphant Abraham with bread and wine, as he was 'a priest of God Most High' (Genesis 14:18). The perfect sacrifice of this Jesus, the sinless priest, conforms to the mind of God and is acceptable to him.

The resurrection of Jesus vindicates his promises. As the risen Christ tells Mary of Magdala in the garden on